BUSINESS NAME

NAME ....

ADDRESS ....

E-MAIL ....

PHONE ....

COMPANY NAME ....

CITY .... STATE .... ZIP ....

WEBSITE ....

NOTE ....

Tumbler Order Form

Customer _____   Order N _____
Address _____   Order Date _____
Phone _____   Due Date _____
E-mail _____   Delivery By _____

Tumbler Details

Tumbler	Size	Quantity

Rush Order   ☐ Yes   ☐ No

Decals

☐ Name   ☐ Monogram   ☐ Initials

Color _____
Font _____

☐ Quote   ☐ Text   ☐ Image

Color _____
Font _____

Design Details

Design Option	x	Color / Glitter Choices
Solid Color		
Ombre		
Full Glitter		
Half Glitter		

Note

Payment

☐ Cash   ☐ Venmo

☐ Check   ☐ Paypal

☐ Card   ☐ Other

Delivery

☐ Drop Off

☐ Pic Up

☐ Shipping

Pricing

Subtotal _____
Tax _____
Shipping _____
Grand total _____
Deposit _____
Due _____

🥤 Tumbler Order Form 🥤

Customer _____ Order N _____

Address _____ Order Date _____

Phone _____ Due Date _____

E-mail _____ Delivery By _____

Tumbler Details

Tumbler	Size	Quantity

Rush Order   ☐ Yes   ☐ No

Decals

☐ Name   ☐ Monogram   ☐ Initials

Color _____

Font _____

☐ Quote   ☐ Text   ☐ Image

Color _____

Font _____

Design Details

Design Option	x	Color / Glitter Choices
Solid Color		
Ombre		
Full Glitter		
Half Glitter		

Note

Payment

☐ Cash   ☐ Venmo

☐ Check   ☐ Paypal

☐ Card   ☐ Other

Delivery

☐ Drop Off

☐ Pic Up

☐ Shipping

Pricing

Subtotal _____

Tax _____

Shipping _____

Grand total _____

Deposit _____

Due _____

Tumbler Order Form

Customer		Order N
Address		Order Date
Phone		Due Date
E-mail		Delivery By

Tumbler Details

Tumbler	Size	Quantity

Rush Order □ Yes □ No

Decals

□ Name   □ Monogram   □ Initials

Color

Font

□ Quote   □ Text   □ Image

Color

Font

Design Details

Design Option	x	Color / Glitter Choices
Solid Color		
Ombre		
Full Glitter		
Half Glitter		

Note

Payment

□ Cash	□ Venmo
□ Check	□ Paypal
□ Card	□ Other

Delivery

□ Drop Off

□ Pic Up

□ Shipping

Pricing

Subtotal

Tax

Shipping

Grand total

Deposit

Due

Tumbler Order Form

Customer _____ Order N _____

Address _____ Order Date _____

Phone _____ Due Date _____

E-mail _____ Delivery By _____

Tumbler Details

Tumbler	Size	Quantity

Rush Order ☐ Yes ☐ No

Decals

☐ Name ☐ Monogram ☐ Initials

_____

Color _____

Font _____

☐ Quote ☐ Text ☐ Image

_____

Color _____

Font _____

Design Details

Design Option	x	Color / Glitter Choices
Solid Color		
Ombre		
Full Glitter		
Half Glitter		

Note

Payment

☐ Cash ☐ Venmo

☐ Check ☐ Paypal

☐ Card ☐ Other

Delivery

☐ Drop Off

☐ Pic Up

☐ Shipping

Pricing

Subtotal _____

Tax _____

Shipping _____

Grand total _____

Deposit _____

Due _____

Tumbler Order Form

Customer _____ Order N _____

Address _____ Order Date _____

Phone _____ Due Date _____

E-mail _____ Delivery By _____

Tumbler Details

Tumbler	Size	Quantity

Rush Order   ☐ Yes   ☐ No

Decals

☐ Name   ☐ Monogram   ☐ Initials

Color _____

Font _____

☐ Quote   ☐ Text   ☐ Image

Color _____

Font _____

Design Details

Design Option	x	Color / Glitter Choices
Solid Color		
Ombre		
Full Glitter		
Half Glitter		

Note

_____

_____

_____

_____

_____

_____

_____

Payment

☐ Cash   ☐ Venmo

☐ Check   ☐ Paypal

☐ Card   ☐ Other

Delivery

☐ Drop Off

☐ Pic Up

☐ Shipping

Pricing

Subtotal _____

Tax _____

Shipping _____

Grand total _____

Deposit _____

Due _____

Tumbler Order Form

Customer _____   Order N _____

Address _____   Order Date _____

Phone _____   Due Date _____

E-mail _____   Delivery By _____

Tumbler Details

Tumbler	Size	Quantity

Rush Order   ☐ Yes   ☐ No

Decals

☐ Name   ☐ Monogram   ☐ Initials
_____
Color _____
Font _____

☐ Quote   ☐ Text   ☐ Image
_____
Color _____
Font _____

Design Details

Design Option	x	Color / Glitter Choices
Solid Color		
Ombre		
Full Glitter		
Half Glitter		

Note

Payment

☐ Cash   ☐ Venmo

☐ Check   ☐ Paypal

☐ Card   ☐ Other

Delivery

☐ Drop Off

☐ Pic Up

☐ Shipping

Pricing

Subtotal _____

Tax _____

Shipping _____

Grand total _____

Deposit _____

Due _____

Tumbler Order Form

Customer _____   Order N _____
Address _____   Order Date _____
Phone _____   Due Date _____
E-mail _____   Delivery By _____

Tumbler Details

Tumbler	Size	Quantity

Rush Order   ☐ Yes   ☐ No

Decals

☐ Name   ☐ Monogram   ☐ Initials

Color _____
Font _____

☐ Quote   ☐ Text   ☐ Image

Color _____
Font _____

Design Details

Design Option	x	Color / Glitter Choices
Solid Color		
Ombre		
Full Glitter		
Half Glitter		

Note

Payment

☐ Cash   ☐ Venmo
☐ Check   ☐ Paypal
☐ Card   ☐ Other

Delivery

☐ Drop Off
☐ Pic Up
☐ Shipping

Pricing

Subtotal _____
Tax _____
Shipping _____
Grand total _____
Deposit _____
Due _____

Tumbler Order Form

Customer _____ Order N _____

Address _____ Order Date _____

Phone _____ Due Date _____

E-mail _____ Delivery By _____

Tumbler Details

Tumbler	Size	Quantity

Rush Order ☐ Yes ☐ No

Decals

☐ Name ☐ Monogram ☐ Initials

Color _____

Font _____

☐ Quote ☐ Text ☐ Image

Color _____

Font _____

Design Details

Design Option	x	Color / Glitter Choices
Solid Color		
Ombre		
Full Glitter		
Half Glitter		

Note

Payment

☐ Cash ☐ Venmo

☐ Check ☐ Paypal

☐ Card ☐ Other

Delivery

☐ Drop Off

☐ Pic Up

☐ Shipping

Pricing

Subtotal _____

Tax _____

Shipping _____

Grand total _____

Deposit _____

Due _____

Tumbler Order Form

Customer _____   Order N _____
Address _____   Order Date _____
Phone _____   Due Date _____
E-mail _____   Delivery By _____

Tumbler Details

Tumbler	Size	Quantity

Rush Order   ☐ Yes   ☐ No

Decals

☐ Name   ☐ Monogram   ☐ Initials

Color _____

Font _____

☐ Quote   ☐ Text   ☐ Image

Color _____

Font _____

Design Details

Design Option	x	Color / Glitter Choices
Solid Color		
Ombre		
Full Glitter		
Half Glitter		

Note

Payment

☐ Cash   ☐ Venmo

☐ Check   ☐ Paypal

☐ Card   ☐ Other

Delivery

☐ Drop Off

☐ Pic Up

☐ Shipping

Pricing

Subtotal _____
Tax _____
Shipping _____
Grand total _____
Deposit _____
Due _____

Tumbler Order Form

Customer _____   Order N _____
Address _____   Order Date _____
Phone _____   Due Date _____
E-mail _____   Delivery By _____

Tumbler Details

Tumbler	Size	Quantity

Rush Order   ☐ Yes   ☐ No

Decals

☐ Name   ☐ Monogram   ☐ Initials

Color _____
Font _____

☐ Quote   ☐ Text   ☐ Image

Color _____
Font _____

Design Details

Design Option	x	Color / Glitter Choices
Solid Color		
Ombre		
Full Glitter		
Half Glitter		

Note

Payment

☐ Cash   ☐ Venmo
☐ Check   ☐ Paypal
☐ Card   ☐ Other

Delivery

☐ Drop Off
☐ Pic Up
☐ Shipping

Pricing

Subtotal _____
Tax _____
Shipping _____
Grand total _____
Deposit _____
Due _____

Tumbler Order Form

Customer _____ Order N _____

Address _____ Order Date _____

Phone _____ Due Date _____

E-mail _____ Delivery By _____

Tumbler Details

Tumbler	Size	Quantity

Rush Order ☐ Yes ☐ No

Decals

☐ Name ☐ Monogram ☐ Initials

Color _____

Font _____

☐ Quote ☐ Text ☐ Image

Color _____

Font _____

Design Details

Design Option	x	Color / Glitter Choices
Solid Color		
Ombre		
Full Glitter		
Half Glitter		

Note

_____

_____

_____

_____

_____

_____

_____

Payment

☐ Cash ☐ Venmo

☐ Check ☐ Paypal

☐ Card ☐ Other

Delivery

☐ Drop Off

☐ Pic Up

☐ Shipping

Pricing

Subtotal _____

Tax _____

Shipping _____

Grand total _____

Deposit _____

Due _____

Tumbler Order Form

Customer		Order N	
Address		Order Date	
Phone		Due Date	
E-mail		Delivery By	

Tumbler Details

Tumbler	Size	Quantity

Rush Order ☐ Yes ☐ No

Decals

☐ Name   ☐ Monogram   ☐ Initials

Color

Font

☐ Quote   ☐ Text   ☐ Image

Color

Font

Design Details

Design Option	x	Color / Glitter Choices
Solid Color		
Ombre		
Full Glitter		
Half Glitter		

Note

Payment

☐ Cash   ☐ Venmo

☐ Check   ☐ Paypal

☐ Card   ☐ Other

Delivery

☐ Drop Off

☐ Pic Up

☐ Shipping

Pricing

Subtotal

Tax

Shipping

Grand total

Deposit

Due

Tumbler Order Form

Customer _____ Order N _____

Address _____ Order Date _____

Phone _____ Due Date _____

E-mail _____ Delivery By _____

Tumbler Details

Tumbler	Size	Quantity

Rush Order □ Yes □ No

Decals

□ Name □ Monogram □ Initials

Color _____

Font _____

□ Quote □ Text □ Image

Color _____

Font _____

Design Details

Design Option	x	Color / Glitter Choices
Solid Color		
Ombre		
Full Glitter		
Half Glitter		

Note

Payment

□ Cash   □ Venmo

□ Check □ Paypal

□ Card   □ Other

Delivery

□ Drop Off

□ Pic Up

□ Shipping

Pricing

Subtotal _____

Tax _____

Shipping _____

Grand total _____

Deposit _____

Due _____

Tumbler Order Form

Customer _____   Order N _____
Address _____   Order Date _____
Phone _____   Due Date _____
E-mail _____   Delivery By _____

Tumbler Details

Tumbler	Size	Quantity

Rush Order   ☐ Yes   ☐ No

Decals

☐ Name   ☐ Monogram   ☐ Initials

Color _____
Font _____

☐ Quote   ☐ Text   ☐ Image

Color _____
Font _____

Design Details

Design Option	x	Color / Glitter Choices
Solid Color		
Ombre		
Full Glitter		
Half Glitter		

Note

Payment

☐ Cash   ☐ Venmo

☐ Check   ☐ Paypal

☐ Card   ☐ Other

Delivery

☐ Drop Off

☐ Pic Up

☐ Shipping

Pricing

Subtotal _____
Tax _____
Shipping _____
Grand total _____
Deposit _____
Due _____

🥤 *Tumbler Order Form* 🥤

Customer _____   Order N _____
Address _____   Order Date _____
Phone _____   Due Date _____
E-mail _____   Delivery By _____

Tumbler Details

Tumbler	Size	Quantity

Rush Order   ☐ Yes   ☐ No

Decals

☐ Name   ☐ Monogram   ☐ Initials
_____

Color _____
Font _____

☐ Quote   ☐ Text   ☐ Image
_____

Color _____
Font _____

Design Details

Design Option	x	Color / Glitter Choices
Solid Color		
Ombre		
Full Glitter		
Half Glitter		

Note

Payment

☐ Cash   ☐ Venmo

☐ Check   ☐ Paypal

☐ Card   ☐ Other

Delivery

☐ Drop Off

☐ Pic Up

☐ Shipping

Pricing

Subtotal _____
Tax _____
Shipping _____
Grand total _____
Deposit _____
Due _____

Tumbler Order Form

Customer _____ Order N _____

Address _____ Order Date _____

Phone _____ Due Date _____

E-mail _____ Delivery By _____

Tumbler Details

Tumbler	Size	Quantity

Rush Order   ☐ Yes   ☐ No

Decals

☐ Name   ☐ Monogram   ☐ Initials

Color _____

Font _____

☐ Quote   ☐ Text   ☐ Image

Color _____

Font _____

Design Details

Design Option	x	Color / Glitter Choices
Solid Color		
Ombre		
Full Glitter		
Half Glitter		

Note

Payment

☐ Cash   ☐ Venmo

☐ Check   ☐ Paypal

☐ Card   ☐ Other

Delivery

☐ Drop Off

☐ Pic Up

☐ Shipping

Pricing

Subtotal _____

Tax _____

Shipping _____

Grand total _____

Deposit _____

Due _____

🥤 Tumbler Order Form 🥤

Customer	Order N	
Address	Order Date	
Phone	Due Date	
E-mail	Delivery By	

Tumbler Details

Tumbler	Size	Quantity

Rush Order ☐ Yes   ☐ No

Decals

☐ Name   ☐ Monogram   ☐ Initials

Color

Font

☐ Quote   ☐ Text   ☐ Image

Color

Font

Design Details

Design Option	x	Color / Glitter Choices
Solid Color		
Ombre		
Full Glitter		
Half Glitter		

Note

Payment

☐ Cash   ☐ Venmo

☐ Check   ☐ Paypal

☐ Card   ☐ Other

Delivery

☐ Drop Off

☐ Pic Up

☐ Shipping

Pricing

Subtotal

Tax

Shipping

Grand total

Deposit

Due

🥤 *Tumbler Order Form* 🥤

Customer		Order N
Address		Order Date
Phone		Due Date
E-mail		Delivery By

Tumbler Details

Tumbler	Size	Quantity

Rush Order   ☐ Yes   ☐ No

Decals

☐ Name   ☐ Monogram   ☐ Initials

Color

Font

☐ Quote   ☐ Text   ☐ Image

Color

Font

Design Details

Design Option	x	Color / Glitter Choices
Solid Color		
Ombre		
Full Glitter		
Half Glitter		

Note

Payment

☐ Cash   ☐ Venmo

☐ Check   ☐ Paypal

☐ Card   ☐ Other

Delivery

☐ Drop Off

☐ Pic Up

☐ Shipping

Pricing

Subtotal

Tax

Shipping

Grand total

Deposit

Due

Tumbler Order Form

Customer _____   Order N _____
Address _____   Order Date _____
Phone _____   Due Date _____
E-mail _____   Delivery By _____

Tumbler Details

Tumbler	Size	Quantity

Rush Order   ☐ Yes   ☐ No

Decals

☐ Name ☐ Monogram ☐ Initials

Color _____
Font _____

☐ Quote   ☐ Text   ☐ Image

Color _____
Font _____

Design Details

Design Option	x	Color / Glitter Choices
Solid Color		
Ombre		
Full Glitter		
Half Glitter		

Note

Payment

☐ Cash   ☐ Venmo
☐ Check   ☐ Paypal
☐ Card   ☐ Other

Delivery

☐ Drop Off
☐ Pic Up
☐ Shipping

Pricing

Subtotal _____
Tax _____
Shipping _____
Grand total _____
Deposit _____
Due _____

Tumbler Order Form

Customer _____   Order N _____
Address _____   Order Date _____
Phone _____   Due Date _____
E-mail _____   Delivery By _____

Tumbler Details

Tumbler	Size	Quantity

Rush Order   ☐ Yes   ☐ No

Decals

☐ Name   ☐ Monogram   ☐ Initials

Color _____

Font _____

☐ Quote   ☐ Text   ☐ Image

Color _____

Font _____

Design Details

Design Option	x	Color / Glitter Choices
Solid Color		
Ombre		
Full Glitter		
Half Glitter		

Note

Payment

☐ Cash   ☐ Venmo

☐ Check   ☐ Paypal

☐ Card   ☐ Other

Delivery

☐ Drop Off

☐ Pic Up

☐ Shipping

Pricing

Subtotal _____
Tax _____
Shipping _____
Grand total _____
Deposit _____
Due _____

🥤 Tumbler Order Form 🥤

Customer _____ Order N _____

Address _____ Order Date _____

Phone _____ Due Date _____

E-mail _____ Delivery By _____

Tumbler Details

Tumbler	Size	Quantity

Rush Order   ☐ Yes   ☐ No

Decals

☐ Name   ☐ Monogram   ☐ Initials

Color _____

Font _____

☐ Quote   ☐ Text   ☐ Image

Color _____

Font _____

Design Details

Design Option	x	Color / Glitter Choices
Solid Color		
Ombre		
Full Glitter		
Half Glitter		

Note

Payment

☐ Cash   ☐ Venmo

☐ Check   ☐ Paypal

☐ Card   ☐ Other

Delivery

☐ Drop Off

☐ Pic Up

☐ Shipping

Pricing

Subtotal _____

Tax _____

Shipping _____

Grand total _____

Deposit _____

Due _____

Tumbler Order Form

Customer _____	Order N _____
Address _____	Order Date _____
Phone _____	Due Date _____
E-mail _____	Delivery By _____

Tumbler Details

Tumbler	Size	Quantity

Rush Order ☐ Yes   ☐ No

Decals

☐ Name   ☐ Monogram   ☐ Initials

Color _____

Font _____

☐ Quote   ☐ Text   ☐ Image

Color _____

Font _____

Design Details

Design Option	x	Color / Glitter Choices
Solid Color		
Ombre		
Full Glitter		
Half Glitter		

Note

Payment

☐ Cash	☐ Venmo
☐ Check	☐ Paypal
☐ Card	☐ Other

Delivery

☐ Drop Off

☐ Pic Up

☐ Shipping

Pricing

Subtotal _____

Tax _____

Shipping _____

Grand total _____

Deposit _____

Due _____

Tumbler Order Form

Customer _____ Order N _____

Address _____ Order Date _____

Phone _____ Due Date _____

E-mail _____ Delivery By _____

Tumbler Details

Tumbler	Size	Quantity

Rush Order ☐ Yes ☐ No

Decals

☐ Name ☐ Monogram ☐ Initials

_____

Color _____

Font _____

☐ Quote ☐ Text ☐ Image

_____

Color _____

Font _____

Design Details

Design Option	x	Color / Glitter Choices
Solid Color		
Ombre		
Full Glitter		
Half Glitter		

Note

Payment

☐ Cash ☐ Venmo

☐ Check ☐ Paypal

☐ Card ☐ Other

Delivery

☐ Drop Off

☐ Pic Up

☐ Shipping

Pricing

Subtotal _____

Tax _____

Shipping _____

Grand total _____

Deposit _____

Due _____

Tumbler Order Form

Customer _____ Order N _____
Address _____ Order Date _____
Phone _____ Due Date _____
E-mail _____ Delivery By _____

Tumbler Details

Tumbler	Size	Quantity

Rush Order   ☐ Yes   ☐ No

Decals

☐ Name   ☐ Monogram   ☐ Initials

Color _____
Font _____

☐ Quote   ☐ Text   ☐ Image

Color _____
Font _____

Design Details

Design Option	x	Color / Glitter Choices
Solid Color		
Ombre		
Full Glitter		
Half Glitter		

Note

Payment

☐ Cash   ☐ Venmo

☐ Check   ☐ Paypal

☐ Card   ☐ Other

Delivery

☐ Drop Off

☐ Pic Up

☐ Shipping

Pricing

Subtotal _____
Tax _____
Shipping _____
Grand total _____
Deposit _____
Due _____

Tumbler Order Form

Customer	_____		Order N	_____
Address	_____		Order Date	_____
Phone	_____		Due Date	_____
E-mail	_____		Delivery By	_____

Tumbler Details

Tumbler	Size	Quantity

Rush Order   ☐ Yes   ☐ No

Decals

☐ Name   ☐ Monogram   ☐ Initials

Color _____

Font _____

☐ Quote   ☐ Text   ☐ Image

Color _____

Font _____

Design Details

Design Option	x	Color / Glitter Choices
Solid Color		
Ombre		
Full Glitter		
Half Glitter		

Note

Payment

☐ Cash   ☐ Venmo

☐ Check   ☐ Paypal

☐ Card   ☐ Other

Delivery

☐ Drop Off

☐ Pic Up

☐ Shipping

Pricing

Subtotal	_____
Tax	_____
Shipping	_____
Grand total	_____
Deposit	_____
Due	_____

Tumbler Order Form

Customer _____   Order N _____

Address _____   Order Date _____

Phone _____   Due Date _____

E-mail _____   Delivery By _____

Tumbler Details

Tumbler	Size	Quantity

Rush Order   ☐ Yes   ☐ No

Decals

☐ Name   ☐ Monogram   ☐ Initials

Color _____

Font _____

☐ Quote   ☐ Text   ☐ Image

Color _____

Font _____

Design Details

Design Option	x	Color / Glitter Choices
Solid Color		
Ombre		
Full Glitter		
Half Glitter		

Note

Payment

☐ Cash   ☐ Venmo

☐ Check   ☐ Paypal

☐ Card   ☐ Other

Delivery

☐ Drop Off

☐ Pic Up

☐ Shipping

Pricing

Subtotal _____

Tax _____

Shipping _____

Grand total _____

Deposit _____

Due _____

Tumbler Order Form

Customer	Order N
Address	Order Date
Phone	Due Date
E-mail	Delivery By

Tumbler Details

Tumbler	Size	Quantity

Rush Order ☐ Yes ☐ No

Decals

☐ Name ☐ Monogram ☐ Initials

Color

Font

☐ Quote ☐ Text ☐ Image

Color

Font

Design Details

Design Option	x	Color / Glitter Choices
Solid Color		
Ombre		
Full Glitter		
Half Glitter		

Note

Payment

☐ Cash ☐ Venmo

☐ Check ☐ Paypal

☐ Card ☐ Other

Delivery

☐ Drop Off

☐ Pic Up

☐ Shipping

Pricing

Subtotal	
Tax	
Shipping	
Grand total	
Deposit	
Due	

Tumbler Order Form

Customer _____ Order N _____
Address _____ Order Date _____
Phone _____ Due Date _____
E-mail _____ Delivery By _____

Tumbler Details

Tumbler	Size	Quantity

Rush Order   ☐ Yes   ☐ No

Decals

☐ Name   ☐ Monogram   ☐ Initials

Color _____
Font _____

☐ Quote   ☐ Text   ☐ Image

Color _____
Font _____

Design Details

Design Option	x	Color / Glitter Choices
Solid Color		
Ombre		
Full Glitter		
Half Glitter		

Note

Payment

☐ Cash   ☐ Venmo
☐ Check   ☐ Paypal
☐ Card   ☐ Other

Delivery

☐ Drop Off
☐ Pic Up
☐ Shipping

Pricing

Subtotal _____
Tax _____
Shipping _____
Grand total _____
Deposit _____
Due _____

Tumbler Order Form

Customer		Order N
Address		Order Date
Phone		Due Date
E-mail		Delivery By

Tumbler Details

Tumbler	Size	Quantity

Rush Order ☐ Yes   ☐ No

Decals

☐ Name   ☐ Monogram   ☐ Initials

Color

Font

☐ Quote   ☐ Text   ☐ Image

Color

Font

Design Details

Design Option	x	Color / Glitter Choices
Solid Color		
Ombre		
Full Glitter		
Half Glitter		

Note

Payment

☐ Cash	☐ Venmo
☐ Check	☐ Paypal
☐ Card	☐ Other

Delivery

☐ Drop Off

☐ Pic Up

☐ Shipping

Pricing

Subtotal

Tax

Shipping

Grand total

Deposit

Due

Tumbler Order Form

Customer _____ Order N _____

Address _____ Order Date _____

Phone _____ Due Date _____

E-mail _____ Delivery By _____

Tumbler Details

Tumbler	Size	Quantity

Rush Order   ☐ Yes   ☐ No

Decals

☐ Name   ☐ Monogram   ☐ Initials

Color _____

Font _____

☐ Quote   ☐ Text   ☐ Image

Color _____

Font _____

Design Details

Design Option	x	Color / Glitter Choices
Solid Color		
Ombre		
Full Glitter		
Half Glitter		

Note

Payment

☐ Cash   ☐ Venmo

☐ Check   ☐ Paypal

☐ Card   ☐ Other

Delivery

☐ Drop Off

☐ Pic Up

☐ Shipping

Pricing

Subtotal _____

Tax _____

Shipping _____

Grand total _____

Deposit _____

Due _____

Tumbler Order Form

Customer _____ Order N _____

Address _____ Order Date _____

Phone _____ Due Date _____

E-mail _____ Delivery By _____

Tumbler Details

Tumbler	Size	Quantity

Rush Order ☐ Yes ☐ No

Decals

☐ Name ☐ Monogram ☐ Initials

Color _____

Font _____

☐ Quote ☐ Text ☐ Image

Color _____

Font _____

Design Details

Design Option	x	Color / Glitter Choices
Solid Color		
Ombre		
Full Glitter		
Half Glitter		

Note

Payment

☐ Cash ☐ Venmo

☐ Check ☐ Paypal

☐ Card ☐ Other

Delivery

☐ Drop Off

☐ Pic Up

☐ Shipping

Pricing

Subtotal _____

Tax _____

Shipping _____

Grand total _____

Deposit _____

Due _____

Tumbler Order Form

Customer _____ Order N _____

Address _____ Order Date _____

Phone _____ Due Date _____

E-mail _____ Delivery By _____

Tumbler Details

Tumbler	Size	Quantity

Rush Order   ☐ Yes   ☐ No

Decals

☐ Name   ☐ Monogram   ☐ Initials

Color _____

Font _____

☐ Quote   ☐ Text   ☐ Image

Color _____

Font _____

Design Details

Design Option	x	Color / Glitter Choices
Solid Color		
Ombre		
Full Glitter		
Half Glitter		

Note

Payment

☐ Cash   ☐ Venmo

☐ Check   ☐ Paypal

☐ Card   ☐ Other

Delivery

☐ Drop Off

☐ Pic Up

☐ Shipping

Pricing

Subtotal _____

Tax _____

Shipping _____

Grand total _____

Deposit _____

Due _____

Tumbler Order Form

Customer		Order N	
Address		Order Date	
Phone		Due Date	
E-mail		Delivery By	

Tumbler Details

Tumbler	Size	Quantity

Rush Order   □ Yes   □ No

Decals

□ Name   □ Monogram   □ Initials

Color _____

Font _____

□ Quote   □ Text   □ Image

Color _____

Font _____

Design Details

Design Option	x	Color / Glitter Choices
Solid Color		
Ombre		
Full Glitter		
Half Glitter		

Note

Payment

□ Cash   □ Venmo

□ Check   □ Paypal

□ Card   □ Other

Delivery

□ Drop Off

□ Pic Up

□ Shipping

Pricing

Subtotal	
Tax	
Shipping	
Grand total	
Deposit	
Due	

Tumbler Order Form

Customer _____   Order N _____
Address _____   Order Date _____
Phone _____   Due Date _____
E-mail _____   Delivery By _____

Tumbler Details

Tumbler	Size	Quantity

Rush Order   ☐ Yes   ☐ No

Decals

☐ Name   ☐ Monogram   ☐ Initials

Color _____
Font _____

☐ Quote   ☐ Text   ☐ Image

Color _____
Font _____

Design Details

Design Option	x	Color / Glitter Choices
Solid Color		
Ombre		
Full Glitter		
Half Glitter		

Note

Payment

☐ Cash   ☐ Venmo

☐ Check   ☐ Paypal

☐ Card   ☐ Other

Delivery

☐ Drop Off

☐ Pic Up

☐ Shipping

Pricing

Subtotal _____
Tax _____
Shipping _____
Grand total _____
Deposit _____
Due _____

🥤 Tumbler Order Form 🥤

Customer		Order N
Address		Order Date
Phone		Due Date
E-mail		Delivery By

Tumbler Details

Tumbler	Size	Quantity

Rush Order ☐ Yes   ☐ No

Decals

☐ Name   ☐ Monogram   ☐ Initials

Color

Font

☐ Quote   ☐ Text   ☐ Image

Color

Font

Design Details

Design Option	x	Color / Glitter Choices
Solid Color		
Ombre		
Full Glitter		
Half Glitter		

Note

Payment

☐ Cash   ☐ Venmo

☐ Check   ☐ Paypal

☐ Card   ☐ Other

Delivery

☐ Drop Off

☐ Pic Up

☐ Shipping

Pricing

Subtotal	
Tax	
Shipping	
Grand total	
Deposit	
Due	

Tumbler Order Form

Customer _____ Order N _____

Address _____ Order Date _____

Phone _____ Due Date _____

E-mail _____ Delivery By _____

Tumbler Details

Tumbler	Size	Quantity

Rush Order   ☐ Yes   ☐ No

Decals

☐ Name   ☐ Monogram   ☐ Initials

Color _____

Font _____

☐ Quote   ☐ Text   ☐ Image

Color _____

Font _____

Design Details

Design Option	x	Color / Glitter Choices
Solid Color		
Ombre		
Full Glitter		
Half Glitter		

Note

Payment

☐ Cash   ☐ Venmo

☐ Check   ☐ Paypal

☐ Card   ☐ Other

Delivery

☐ Drop Off

☐ Pic Up

☐ Shipping

Pricing

Subtotal _____

Tax _____

Shipping _____

Grand total _____

Deposit _____

Due _____

Tumbler Order Form

Customer _____ Order N _____

Address _____ Order Date _____

Phone _____ Due Date _____

E-mail _____ Delivery By _____

Tumbler Details

Tumbler	Size	Quantity

Rush Order   ☐ Yes   ☐ No

Decals

☐ Name   ☐ Monogram   ☐ Initials

Color _____

Font _____

☐ Quote   ☐ Text   ☐ Image

Color _____

Font _____

Design Details

Design Option	x	Color / Glitter Choices
Solid Color		
Ombre		
Full Glitter		
Half Glitter		

Note

Payment

☐ Cash   ☐ Venmo

☐ Check   ☐ Paypal

☐ Card   ☐ Other

Delivery

☐ Drop Off

☐ Pic Up

☐ Shipping

Pricing

Subtotal _____

Tax _____

Shipping _____

Grand total _____

Deposit _____

Due _____

Tumbler Order Form

Customer _____ Order N _____
Address _____ Order Date _____
Phone _____ Due Date _____
E-mail _____ Delivery By _____

Tumbler Details

Tumbler	Size	Quantity

Rush Order   ☐ Yes   ☐ No

Decals

☐ Name   ☐ Monogram   ☐ Initials

Color _____
Font _____

☐ Quote   ☐ Text   ☐ Image

Color _____
Font _____

Design Details

Design Option	x	Color / Glitter Choices
Solid Color		
Ombre		
Full Glitter		
Half Glitter		

Note

_____
_____
_____
_____
_____
_____
_____

Payment

☐ Cash   ☐ Venmo

☐ Check   ☐ Paypal

☐ Card   ☐ Other

Delivery

☐ Drop Off

☐ Pic Up

☐ Shipping

Pricing

Subtotal _____
Tax _____
Shipping _____
Grand total _____
Deposit _____
Due _____

Tumbler Order Form

Customer _____   Order N _____
Address _____   Order Date _____
Phone _____   Due Date _____
E-mail _____   Delivery By _____

Tumbler Details

Tumbler	Size	Quantity

Rush Order   ☐ Yes   ☐ No

Decals

☐ Name   ☐ Monogram   ☐ Initials

Color _____
Font _____

☐ Quote   ☐ Text   ☐ Image

Color _____
Font _____

Design Details

Design Option	x	Color / Glitter Choices
Solid Color		
Ombre		
Full Glitter		
Half Glitter		

Note

Payment

☐ Cash   ☐ Venmo

☐ Check   ☐ Paypal

☐ Card   ☐ Other

Delivery

☐ Drop Off

☐ Pic Up

☐ Shipping

Pricing

Subtotal _____
Tax _____
Shipping _____
Grand total _____
Deposit _____
Due _____

Tumbler Order Form

Customer _____ Order N _____
Address _____ Order Date _____
Phone _____ Due Date _____
E-mail _____ Delivery By _____

Tumbler Details

Tumbler	Size	Quantity

Rush Order   ☐ Yes   ☐ No

Decals

☐ Name   ☐ Monogram   ☐ Initials

Color _____
Font _____

☐ Quote   ☐ Text   ☐ Image

Color _____
Font _____

Design Details

Design Option	x	Color / Glitter Choices
Solid Color		
Ombre		
Full Glitter		
Half Glitter		

Note

Payment

☐ Cash   ☐ Venmo
☐ Check   ☐ Paypal
☐ Card   ☐ Other

Delivery

☐ Drop Off
☐ Pic Up
☐ Shipping

Pricing

Subtotal _____
Tax _____
Shipping _____
Grand total _____
Deposit _____
Due _____

Tumbler Order Form

Customer _____ Order N _____

Address _____ Order Date _____

Phone _____ Due Date _____

E-mail _____ Delivery By _____

Tumbler Details

Tumbler	Size	Quantity

Rush Order   □ Yes   □ No

Decals

□ Name   □ Monogram   □ Initials

Color _____

Font _____

□ Quote   □ Text   □ Image

Color _____

Font _____

Design Details

Design Option	x	Color / Glitter Choices
Solid Color		
Ombre		
Full Glitter		
Half Glitter		

Note

Payment

□ Cash   □ Venmo

□ Check   □ Paypal

□ Card   □ Other

Delivery

□ Drop Off

□ Pic Up

□ Shipping

Pricing

Subtotal _____

Tax _____

Shipping _____

Grand total _____

Deposit _____

Due _____

Tumbler Order Form

Customer		Order N
Address		Order Date
Phone		Due Date
E-mail		Delivery By

Tumbler Details

Tumbler	Size	Quantity

Rush Order   ☐ Yes   ☐ No

Decals

☐ Name   ☐ Monogram   ☐ Initials

Color
Font

☐ Quote   ☐ Text   ☐ Image

Color
Font

Design Details

Design Option	x	Color / Glitter Choices
Solid Color		
Ombre		
Full Glitter		
Half Glitter		

Note

Payment

☐ Cash   ☐ Venmo

☐ Check   ☐ Paypal

☐ Card   ☐ Other

Delivery

☐ Drop Off

☐ Pic Up

☐ Shipping

Pricing

Subtotal
Tax
Shipping
Grand total
Deposit
Due

Tumbler Order Form

Customer _____ Order N _____
Address _____ Order Date _____
Phone _____ Due Date _____
E-mail _____ Delivery By _____

Tumbler Details

Tumbler	Size	Quantity

Rush Order ☐ Yes   ☐ No

Decals

☐ Name   ☐ Monogram   ☐ Initials

Color _____
Font _____

☐ Quote   ☐ Text   ☐ Image

Color _____
Font _____

Design Details

Design Option	x	Color / Glitter Choices
Solid Color		
Ombre		
Full Glitter		
Half Glitter		

Note

Payment

☐ Cash   ☐ Venmo

☐ Check   ☐ Paypal

☐ Card   ☐ Other

Delivery

☐ Drop Off

☐ Pic Up

☐ Shipping

Pricing

Subtotal _____
Tax _____
Shipping _____
Grand total _____
Deposit _____
Due _____

Tumbler Order Form

Customer _____ Order N _____

Address _____ Order Date _____

Phone _____ Due Date _____

E-mail _____ Delivery By _____

Tumbler Details

Tumbler	Size	Quantity

Rush Order   ☐ Yes   ☐ No

Decals

☐ Name   ☐ Monogram   ☐ Initials

Color _____

Font _____

☐ Quote   ☐ Text   ☐ Image

Color _____

Font _____

Design Details

Design Option	x	Color / Glitter Choices
Solid Color		
Ombre		
Full Glitter		
Half Glitter		

Note

Payment

☐ Cash   ☐ Venmo

☐ Check   ☐ Paypal

☐ Card   ☐ Other

Delivery

☐ Drop Off

☐ Pic Up

☐ Shipping

Pricing

Subtotal _____

Tax _____

Shipping _____

Grand total _____

Deposit _____

Due _____

Tumbler Order Form

Customer _____   Order N _____
Address _____   Order Date _____
Phone _____   Due Date _____
E-mail _____   Delivery By _____

Tumbler Details

Tumbler	Size	Quantity

Rush Order   □ Yes   □ No

Decals

□ Name   □ Monogram   □ Initials

Color _____
Font _____

□ Quote   □ Text   □ Image

_____

Color _____
Font _____

Design Details

Design Option	x	Color / Glitter Choices
Solid Color		
Ombre		
Full Glitter		
Half Glitter		

Note

Payment

□ Cash   □ Venmo

□ Check   □ Paypal

□ Card   □ Other

Delivery

□ Drop Off

□ Pic Up

□ Shipping

Pricing

Subtotal _____
Tax _____
Shipping _____
Grand total _____
Deposit _____
Due _____

Tumbler Order Form

Customer _____ Order N _____

Address _____ Order Date _____

Phone _____ Due Date _____

E-mail _____ Delivery By _____

Tumbler Details

Tumbler	Size	Quantity

Rush Order   □ Yes   □ No

Decals

□ Name   □ Monogram   □ Initials

Color _____

Font _____

□ Quote   □ Text   □ Image

Color _____

Font _____

Design Details

Design Option	x	Color / Glitter Choices
Solid Color		
Ombre		
Full Glitter		
Half Glitter		

Note

Payment

□ Cash   □ Venmo

□ Check   □ Paypal

□ Card   □ Other

Delivery

□ Drop Off

□ Pic Up

□ Shipping

Pricing

Subtotal _____

Tax _____

Shipping _____

Grand total _____

Deposit _____

Due _____

Tumbler Order Form

Customer _____   Order N _____
Address _____   Order Date _____
Phone _____   Due Date _____
E-mail _____   Delivery By _____

Tumbler Details

Tumbler	Size	Quantity

Rush Order   □ Yes   □ No

Decals

□ Name   □ Monogram   □ Initials

Color _____
Font _____

□ Quote   □ Text   □ Image

Color _____
Font _____

Design Details

Design Option	x	Color / Glitter Choices
Solid Color		
Ombre		
Full Glitter		
Half Glitter		

Note

Payment

□ Cash   □ Venmo
□ Check   □ Paypal
□ Card   □ Other

Delivery

□ Drop Off
□ Pic Up
□ Shipping

Pricing

Subtotal _____
Tax _____
Shipping _____
Grand total _____
Deposit _____
Due _____

Tumbler Order Form

Customer _____ Order N _____

Address _____ Order Date _____

Phone _____ Due Date _____

E-mail _____ Delivery By _____

Tumbler Details

Tumbler	Size	Quantity

Rush Order   ☐ Yes   ☐ No

Decals

☐ Name   ☐ Monogram   ☐ Initials

Color _____

Font _____

☐ Quote   ☐ Text   ☐ Image

Color _____

Font _____

Design Details

Design Option	x	Color / Glitter Choices
Solid Color		
Ombre		
Full Glitter		
Half Glitter		

Note

Payment

☐ Cash   ☐ Venmo

☐ Check   ☐ Paypal

☐ Card   ☐ Other

Delivery

☐ Drop Off

☐ Pic Up

☐ Shipping

Pricing

Subtotal _____

Tax _____

Shipping _____

Grand total _____

Deposit _____

Due _____

Tumbler Order Form

Customer _____   Order N _____

Address _____   Order Date _____

Phone _____   Due Date _____

E-mail _____   Delivery By _____

Tumbler Details

Tumbler	Size	Quantity

Rush Order   ☐ Yes   ☐ No

Decals

☐ Name   ☐ Monogram   ☐ Initials

Color _____

Font _____

☐ Quote   ☐ Text   ☐ Image

Color _____

Font _____

Design Details

Design Option	x	Color / Glitter Choices
Solid Color		
Ombre		
Full Glitter		
Half Glitter		

Note

Payment

☐ Cash   ☐ Venmo

☐ Check   ☐ Paypal

☐ Card   ☐ Other

Delivery

☐ Drop Off

☐ Pic Up

☐ Shipping

Pricing

Subtotal _____

Tax _____

Shipping _____

Grand total _____

Deposit _____

Due _____

Tumbler Order Form

Customer _____ Order N _____

Address _____ Order Date _____

Phone _____ Due Date _____

E-mail _____ Delivery By _____

Tumbler Details

Tumbler	Size	Quantity

Rush Order   □ Yes   □ No

Decals

□ Name   □ Monogram   □ Initials

_____

Color _____

Font _____

□ Quote   □ Text   □ Image

_____

Color _____

Font _____

Design Details

Design Option	x	Color / Glitter Choices
Solid Color		
Ombre		
Full Glitter		
Half Glitter		

Note

_____

_____

_____

_____

_____

_____

_____

Payment

□ Cash   □ Venmo

□ Check   □ Paypal

□ Card   □ Other

Delivery

□ Drop Off

□ Pic Up

□ Shipping

Pricing

Subtotal _____

Tax _____

Shipping _____

Grand total _____

Deposit _____

Due _____

🥤 *Tumbler Order Form* 🥤

Customer _____ Order N _____
Address _____ Order Date _____
Phone _____ Due Date _____
E-mail _____ Delivery By _____

Tumbler Details

Tumbler	Size	Quantity

Rush Order   ☐ Yes   ☐ No

Decals

☐ Name   ☐ Monogram   ☐ Initials

Color _____
Font _____

☐ Quote   ☐ Text   ☐ Image

Color _____
Font _____

Design Details

Design Option	x	Color / Glitter Choices
Solid Color		
Ombre		
Full Glitter		
Half Glitter		

Note

_____
_____
_____
_____
_____
_____
_____

Payment

☐ Cash   ☐ Venmo

☐ Check   ☐ Paypal

☐ Card   ☐ Other

Delivery

☐ Drop Off

☐ Pic Up

☐ Shipping

Pricing

Subtotal _____
Tax _____
Shipping _____
Grand total _____
Deposit _____
Due _____

Tumbler Order Form

Customer		Order N	
Address		Order Date	
Phone		Due Date	
E-mail		Delivery By	

Tumbler Details

Tumbler	Size	Quantity

Rush Order ☐ Yes ☐ No

Decals

☐ Name ☐ Monogram ☐ Initials

Color _____

Font _____

☐ Quote ☐ Text ☐ Image

Color _____

Font _____

Design Details

Design Option	x	Color / Glitter Choices
Solid Color		
Ombre		
Full Glitter		
Half Glitter		

Note

Payment

☐ Cash ☐ Venmo

☐ Check ☐ Paypal

☐ Card ☐ Other

Delivery

☐ Drop Off

☐ Pic Up

☐ Shipping

Pricing

Subtotal	
Tax	
Shipping	
Grand total	
Deposit	
Due	

Tumbler Order Form

Customer _____ Order N _____

Address _____ Order Date _____

Phone _____ Due Date _____

E-mail _____ Delivery By _____

Tumbler Details

Tumbler	Size	Quantity

Rush Order   ☐ Yes   ☐ No

Decals

☐ Name   ☐ Monogram   ☐ Initials

Color _____

Font _____

☐ Quote   ☐ Text   ☐ Image

Color _____

Font _____

Design Details

Design Option	x	Color / Glitter Choices
Solid Color		
Ombre		
Full Glitter		
Half Glitter		

Note

Payment

☐ Cash   ☐ Venmo

☐ Check   ☐ Paypal

☐ Card   ☐ Other

Delivery

☐ Drop Off

☐ Pic Up

☐ Shipping

Pricing

Subtotal _____

Tax _____

Shipping _____

Grand total _____

Deposit _____

Due _____

🥤 Tumbler Order Form 🥤

Customer _____	Order N _____
Address _____	Order Date _____
Phone _____	Due Date _____
E-mail _____	Delivery By _____

Tumbler Details

Tumbler	Size	Quantity

Rush Order   ☐ Yes   ☐ No

Decals

☐ Name   ☐ Monogram   ☐ Initials

Color _____

Font _____

☐ Quote   ☐ Text   ☐ Image

Color _____

Font _____

Design Details

Design Option	x	Color / Glitter Choices
Solid Color		
Ombre		
Full Glitter		
Half Glitter		

Note

Payment

☐ Cash   ☐ Venmo

☐ Check   ☐ Paypal

☐ Card   ☐ Other

Delivery

☐ Drop Off

☐ Pic Up

☐ Shipping

Pricing

Subtotal _____

Tax _____

Shipping _____

Grand total _____

Deposit _____

Due _____

Tumbler Order Form

Customer _____ Order N _____

Address _____ Order Date _____

Phone _____ Due Date _____

E-mail _____ Delivery By _____

Tumbler Details

Tumbler	Size	Quantity

Rush Order   ☐ Yes   ☐ No

Decals

☐ Name   ☐ Monogram   ☐ Initials

_____

Color _____

Font _____

☐ Quote   ☐ Text   ☐ Image

_____

Color _____

Font _____

Design Details

Design Option	x	Color / Glitter Choices
Solid Color		
Ombre		
Full Glitter		
Half Glitter		

Note

Payment

☐ Cash   ☐ Venmo

☐ Check   ☐ Paypal

☐ Card   ☐ Other

Delivery

☐ Drop Off

☐ Pic Up

☐ Shipping

Pricing

Subtotal _____

Tax _____

Shipping _____

Grand total _____

Deposit _____

Due _____

Tumbler Order Form

Customer _____   Order N _____

Address _____   Order Date _____

Phone _____   Due Date _____

E-mail _____   Delivery By _____

Tumbler Details

Tumbler	Size	Quantity

Rush Order   ☐ Yes   ☐ No

Decals

☐ Name   ☐ Monogram   ☐ Initials

Color _____

Font _____

☐ Quote   ☐ Text   ☐ Image

Color _____

Font _____

Design Details

Design Option	x	Color / Glitter Choices
Solid Color		
Ombre		
Full Glitter		
Half Glitter		

Note

Payment

☐ Cash   ☐ Venmo

☐ Check   ☐ Paypal

☐ Card   ☐ Other

Delivery

☐ Drop Off

☐ Pic Up

☐ Shipping

Pricing

Subtotal _____

Tax _____

Shipping _____

Grand total _____

Deposit _____

Due _____

Tumbler Order Form

Customer _____ Order N _____

Address _____ Order Date _____

Phone _____ Due Date _____

E-mail _____ Delivery By _____

Tumbler Details

Tumbler	Size	Quantity

Rush Order   □ Yes   □ No

Decals

□ Name   □ Monogram   □ Initials
_____

Color _____

Font _____

□ Quote   □ Text   □ Image
_____

Color _____

Font _____

Design Details

Design Option	x	Color / Glitter Choices
Solid Color		
Ombre		
Full Glitter		
Half Glitter		

Note

Payment

□ Cash   □ Venmo

□ Check   □ Paypal

□ Card   □ Other

Delivery

□ Drop Off

□ Pic Up

□ Shipping

Pricing

Subtotal _____

Tax _____

Shipping _____

Grand total _____

Deposit _____

Due _____

Tumbler Order Form

Customer _____   Order N _____
Address _____   Order Date _____
Phone _____   Due Date _____
E-mail _____   Delivery By _____

Tumbler Details

Tumbler	Size	Quantity

Rush Order   □ Yes   □ No

Decals

□ Name   □ Monogram   □ Initials

Color _____
Font _____

□ Quote   □ Text   □ Image

Color _____
Font _____

Design Details

Design Option	x	Color / Glitter Choices
Solid Color		
Ombre		
Full Glitter		
Half Glitter		

Note

Payment

□ Cash   □ Venmo
□ Check   □ Paypal
□ Card   □ Other

Delivery

□ Drop Off
□ Pic Up
□ Shipping

Pricing

Subtotal _____
Tax _____
Shipping _____
Grand total _____
Deposit _____
Due _____

🥤 Tumbler Order Form 🥤

Customer		Order N
Address		Order Date
Phone		Due Date
E-mail		Delivery By

Tumbler Details

Tumbler	Size	Quantity

Rush Order ☐ Yes ☐ No

Decals

☐ Name ☐ Monogram ☐ Initials

Color

Font

☐ Quote ☐ Text ☐ Image

Color

Font

Design Details

Design Option	x	Color / Glitter Choices
Solid Color		
Ombre		
Full Glitter		
Half Glitter		

Note

Payment

☐ Cash ☐ Venmo

☐ Check ☐ Paypal

☐ Card ☐ Other

Delivery

☐ Drop Off

☐ Pic Up

☐ Shipping

Pricing

Subtotal	
Tax	
Shipping	
Grand total	
Deposit	
Due	

Tumbler Order Form

Customer		Order N
Address		Order Date
Phone		Due Date
E-mail		Delivery By

Tumbler Details

Tumbler	Size	Quantity

Rush Order   ☐ Yes   ☐ No

Decals

☐ Name ☐ Monogram ☐ Initials

Color

Font

☐ Quote   ☐ Text   ☐ Image

Color

Font

Design Details

Design Option	x	Color / Glitter Choices
Solid Color		
Ombre		
Full Glitter		
Half Glitter		

Note

Payment

☐ Cash	☐ Venmo
☐ Check	☐ Paypal
☐ Card	☐ Other

Delivery

☐ Drop Off

☐ Pic Up

☐ Shipping

Pricing

Subtotal

Tax

Shipping

Grand total

Deposit

Due

🥛 Tumbler Order Form 🥛

Customer		Order N
Address		Order Date
Phone		Due Date
E-mail		Delivery By

Tumbler Details

Tumbler	Size	Quantity

Rush Order ☐ Yes ☐ No

Decals

☐ Name ☐ Monogram ☐ Initials

Color _____

Font _____

☐ Quote ☐ Text ☐ Image

Color _____

Font _____

Design Details

Design Option	x	Color / Glitter Choices
Solid Color		
Ombre		
Full Glitter		
Half Glitter		

Note

Payment

☐ Cash ☐ Venmo

☐ Check ☐ Paypal

☐ Card ☐ Other

Delivery

☐ Drop Off

☐ Pic Up

☐ Shipping

Pricing

Subtotal _____

Tax _____

Shipping _____

Grand total _____

Deposit _____

Due _____

🥤 Tumbler Order Form 🥤

Customer		Order N
Address		Order Date
Phone		Due Date
E-mail		Delivery By

Tumbler Details

Tumbler	Size	Quantity

Rush Order ☐ Yes   ☐ No

Decals

☐ Name ☐ Monogram ☐ Initials

Color

Font

☐ Quote   ☐ Text   ☐ Image

Color

Font

Design Details

Design Option	x	Color / Glitter Choices
Solid Color		
Ombre		
Full Glitter		
Half Glitter		

Note

Payment

☐ Cash   ☐ Venmo

☐ Check   ☐ Paypal

☐ Card   ☐ Other

Delivery

☐ Drop Off

☐ Pic Up

☐ Shipping

Pricing

Subtotal

Tax

Shipping

Grand total

Deposit

Due

Tumbler Order Form

Customer _____ Order N _____

Address _____ Order Date _____

Phone _____ Due Date _____

E-mail _____ Delivery By _____

Tumbler Details

Tumbler	Size	Quantity

Rush Order □ Yes □ No

Decals

□ Name □ Monogram □ Initials

Color _____

Font _____

□ Quote □ Text □ Image

Color _____

Font _____

Design Details

Design Option	x	Color / Glitter Choices
Solid Color		
Ombre		
Full Glitter		
Half Glitter		

Note

Payment

□ Cash □ Venmo

□ Check □ Paypal

□ Card □ Other

Delivery

□ Drop Off

□ Pic Up

□ Shipping

Pricing

Subtotal _____

Tax _____

Shipping _____

Grand total _____

Deposit _____

Due _____

Tumbler Order Form

Customer		Order N
Address		Order Date
Phone		Due Date
E-mail		Delivery By

Tumbler Details

Tumbler	Size	Quantity

Rush Order ☐ Yes ☐ No

Decals

☐ Name ☐ Monogram ☐ Initials

Color

Font

☐ Quote ☐ Text ☐ Image

Color

Font

Design Details

Design Option	x	Color / Glitter Choices
Solid Color		
Ombre		
Full Glitter		
Half Glitter		

Note

Payment

☐ Cash	☐ Venmo
☐ Check	☐ Paypal
☐ Card	☐ Other

Delivery

☐ Drop Off

☐ Pic Up

☐ Shipping

Pricing

Subtotal

Tax

Shipping

Grand total

Deposit

Due

Tumbler Order Form

Customer _____ Order N _____

Address _____ Order Date _____

Phone _____ Due Date _____

E-mail _____ Delivery By _____

Tumbler Details

Tumbler	Size	Quantity

Rush Order   ☐ Yes   ☐ No

Decals

☐ Name   ☐ Monogram   ☐ Initials

Color _____

Font _____

☐ Quote   ☐ Text   ☐ Image

Color _____

Font _____

Design Details

Design Option	x	Color / Glitter Choices
Solid Color		
Ombre		
Full Glitter		
Half Glitter		

Note

Payment

☐   Cash   ☐ Venmo

☐   Check   ☐ Paypal

☐   Card   ☐ Other

Delivery

☐ Drop Off

☐ Pic Up

☐ Shipping

Pricing

Subtotal _____

Tax _____

Shipping _____

Grand total _____

Deposit _____

Due _____

Tumbler Order Form

Customer _____ Order N _____

Address _____ Order Date _____

Phone _____ Due Date _____

E-mail _____ Delivery By _____

Tumbler Details

Tumbler	Size	Quantity

Rush Order   ☐ Yes   ☐ No

Decals

☐ Name   ☐ Monogram   ☐ Initials

Color _____

Font _____

☐ Quote   ☐ Text   ☐ Image

Color _____

Font _____

Design Details

Design Option	x	Color / Glitter Choices
Solid Color		
Ombre		
Full Glitter		
Half Glitter		

Note

Payment

☐ Cash   ☐ Venmo

☐ Check   ☐ Paypal

☐ Card   ☐ Other

Delivery

☐ Drop Off

☐ Pic Up

☐ Shipping

Pricing

Subtotal _____

Tax _____

Shipping _____

Grand total _____

Deposit _____

Due _____

Tumbler Order Form

Customer		Order N	
Address		Order Date	
Phone		Due Date	
E-mail		Delivery By	

Tumbler Details

Tumbler	Size	Quantity

Rush Order   ☐ Yes   ☐ No

Decals

☐ Name   ☐ Monogram   ☐ Initials

Color _____

Font _____

☐ Quote   ☐ Text   ☐ Image

Color _____

Font _____

Design Details

Design Option	x	Color / Glitter Choices
Solid Color		
Ombre		
Full Glitter		
Half Glitter		

Note

Payment

☐ Cash   ☐ Venmo

☐ Check   ☐ Paypal

☐ Card   ☐ Other

Delivery

☐ Drop Off

☐ Pic Up

☐ Shipping

Pricing

Subtotal	
Tax	
Shipping	
Grand total	
Deposit	
Due	

Tumbler Order Form

Customer		Order N
Address		Order Date
Phone		Due Date
E-mail		Delivery By

Tumbler Details

Tumbler	Size	Quantity

Rush Order   ☐ Yes   ☐ No

Decals

☐ Name   ☐ Monogram   ☐ Initials

Color

Font

☐ Quote   ☐ Text   ☐ Image

Color

Font

Design Details

Design Option	x	Color / Glitter Choices
Solid Color		
Ombre		
Full Glitter		
Half Glitter		

Note

Payment

☐ Cash   ☐ Venmo

☐ Check   ☐ Paypal

☐ Card   ☐ Other

Delivery

☐ Drop Off

☐ Pic Up

☐ Shipping

Pricing

Subtotal

Tax

Shipping

Grand total

Deposit

Due

Tumbler Order Form

Customer _____ Order N _____

Address _____ Order Date _____

Phone _____ Due Date _____

E-mail _____ Delivery By _____

Tumbler Details

Tumbler	Size	Quantity

Rush Order   □ Yes   □ No

Decals

□ Name   □ Monogram   □ Initials

_____

Color _____

Font _____

□ Quote   □ Text   □ Image

_____

Color _____

Font _____

Design Details

Design Option	x	Color / Glitter Choices
Solid Color		
Ombre		
Full Glitter		
Half Glitter		

Note

Payment

□ Cash   □ Venmo

□ Check   □ Paypal

□ Card   □ Other

Delivery

□ Drop Off

□ Pic Up

□ Shipping

Pricing

Subtotal _____

Tax _____

Shipping _____

Grand total _____

Deposit _____

Due _____

Tumbler Order Form

Customer _____   Order N _____

Address _____   Order Date _____

Phone _____   Due Date _____

E-mail _____   Delivery By _____

Tumbler Details

Tumbler	Size	Quantity

Rush Order   ☐ Yes   ☐ No

Decals

☐ Name   ☐ Monogram   ☐ Initials

_____

Color _____

Font _____

☐ Quote   ☐ Text   ☐ Image

_____

Color _____

Font _____

Design Details

Design Option	x	Color / Glitter Choices
Solid Color		
Ombre		
Full Glitter		
Half Glitter		

Note

Payment

☐ Cash   ☐ Venmo

☐ Check   ☐ Paypal

☐ Card   ☐ Other

Delivery

☐ Drop Off

☐ Pic Up

☐ Shipping

Pricing

Subtotal _____

Tax _____

Shipping _____

Grand total _____

Deposit _____

Due _____

🥤 Tumbler Order Form 🥤

Customer _____   Order N _____

Address _____   Order Date _____

Phone _____   Due Date _____

E-mail _____   Delivery By _____

Tumbler Details

Tumbler	Size	Quantity

Rush Order   ☐ Yes   ☐ No

Decals

☐ Name   ☐ Monogram   ☐ Initials

Color _____

Font _____

☐ Quote   ☐ Text   ☐ Image

Color _____

Font _____

Design Details

Design Option	x	Color / Glitter Choices
Solid Color		
Ombre		
Full Glitter		
Half Glitter		

Note

Payment

☐ Cash   ☐ Venmo

☐ Check   ☐ Paypal

☐ Card   ☐ Other

Delivery

☐ Drop Off

☐ Pic Up

☐ Shipping

Pricing

Subtotal _____

Tax _____

Shipping _____

Grand total _____

Deposit _____

Due _____

Tumbler Order Form

Customer		Order N
Address		Order Date
Phone		Due Date
E-mail		Delivery By

Tumbler Details

Tumbler	Size	Quantity

Rush Order   ☐ Yes   ☐ No

Decals

☐ Name   ☐ Monogram   ☐ Initials

Color

Font

☐ Quote   ☐ Text   ☐ Image

Color

Font

Design Details

Design Option	x	Color / Glitter Choices
Solid Color		
Ombre		
Full Glitter		
Half Glitter		

Note

Payment

☐ Cash   ☐ Venmo

☐ Check   ☐ Paypal

☐ Card   ☐ Other

Delivery

☐ Drop Off

☐ Pic Up

☐ Shipping

Pricing

Subtotal

Tax

Shipping

Grand total

Deposit

Due

Tumbler Order Form

Customer _____ Order N _____

Address _____ Order Date _____

Phone _____ Due Date _____

E-mail _____ Delivery By _____

Tumbler Details

Tumbler	Size	Quantity

Rush Order   ☐ Yes   ☐ No

Decals

☐ Name   ☐ Monogram   ☐ Initials

Color _____

Font _____

☐ Quote   ☐ Text   ☐ Image

Color _____

Font _____

Design Details

Design Option	x	Color / Glitter Choices
Solid Color		
Ombre		
Full Glitter		
Half Glitter		

Note

_____

_____

_____

_____

_____

Payment

☐ Cash   ☐ Venmo

☐ Check   ☐ Paypal

☐ Card   ☐ Other

Delivery

☐ Drop Off

☐ Pic Up

☐ Shipping

Pricing

Subtotal _____

Tax _____

Shipping _____

Grand total _____

Deposit _____

Due _____

Tumbler Order Form

Customer _____   Order N _____
Address _____   Order Date _____
Phone _____   Due Date _____
E-mail _____   Delivery By _____

Tumbler Details

Tumbler	Size	Quantity

Rush Order   □ Yes   □ No

Decals

□ Name   □ Monogram   □ Initials

Color _____

Font _____

□ Quote   □ Text   □ Image

Color _____

Font _____

Design Details

Design Option	x	Color / Glitter Choices
Solid Color		
Ombre		
Full Glitter		
Half Glitter		

Note

Payment

□ Cash	□ Venmo
□ Check	□ Paypal
□ Card	□ Other

Delivery

□ Drop Off

□ Pic Up

□ Shipping

Pricing

Subtotal _____
Tax _____
Shipping _____
Grand total _____
Deposit _____
Due _____

Tumbler Order Form

Customer _____ Order N _____
Address _____ Order Date _____
Phone _____ Due Date _____
E-mail _____ Delivery By _____

Tumbler Details

Tumbler	Size	Quantity

Rush Order □ Yes   □ No

Decals

□ Name   □ Monogram   □ Initials
_____

Color _____
Font _____

□ Quote   □ Text   □ Image
_____

Color _____
Font _____

Design Details

Design Option	x	Color / Glitter Choices
Solid Color		
Ombre		
Full Glitter		
Half Glitter		

Note

Payment

□ Cash   □ Venmo
□ Check   □ Paypal
□ Card   □ Other

Delivery

□ Drop Off
□ Pic Up
□ Shipping

Pricing

Subtotal _____
Tax _____
Shipping _____
Grand total _____
Deposit _____
Due _____

Tumbler Order Form

Customer _____   Order N _____
Address _____   Order Date _____
Phone _____   Due Date _____
E-mail _____   Delivery By _____

Tumbler Details

Tumbler	Size	Quantity

Rush Order   ☐ Yes   ☐ No

Decals

☐ Name   ☐ Monogram   ☐ Initials

Color _____
Font _____

☐ Quote   ☐ Text   ☐ Image

Color _____
Font _____

Design Details

Design Option	x	Color / Glitter Choices
Solid Color		
Ombre		
Full Glitter		
Half Glitter		

Note

Payment

☐ Cash   ☐ Venmo

☐ Check   ☐ Paypal

☐ Card   ☐ Other

Delivery

☐ Drop Off

☐ Pic Up

☐ Shipping

Pricing

Subtotal _____
Tax _____
Shipping _____
Grand total _____
Deposit _____
Due _____

Tumbler Order Form

Customer _____   Order N _____
Address _____   Order Date _____
Phone _____   Due Date _____
E-mail _____   Delivery By _____

Tumbler Details

Tumbler	Size	Quantity

Rush Order   □ Yes   □ No

Decals

□ Name   □ Monogram   □ Initials

Color _____

Font _____

□ Quote   □ Text   □ Image

Color _____

Font _____

Design Details

Design Option	x	Color / Glitter Choices
Solid Color		
Ombre		
Full Glitter		
Half Glitter		

Note

Payment

□ Cash   □ Venmo

□ Check   □ Paypal

□ Card   □ Other

Delivery

□ Drop Off

□ Pic Up

□ Shipping

Pricing

Subtotal _____
Tax _____
Shipping _____
Grand total _____
Deposit _____
Due _____

Tumbler Order Form

Customer _____ Order N _____

Address _____ Order Date _____

Phone _____ Due Date _____

E-mail _____ Delivery By _____

Tumbler Details

Tumbler	Size	Quantity

Rush Order   ☐ Yes   ☐ No

Decals

☐ Name   ☐ Monogram   ☐ Initials

Color _____

Font _____

☐ Quote   ☐ Text   ☐ Image

Color _____

Font _____

Design Details

Design Option	x	Color / Glitter Choices
Solid Color		
Ombre		
Full Glitter		
Half Glitter		

Note

Payment

☐ Cash   ☐ Venmo

☐ Check   ☐ Paypal

☐ Card   ☐ Other

Delivery

☐ Drop Off

☐ Pic Up

☐ Shipping

Pricing

Subtotal _____

Tax _____

Shipping _____

Grand total _____

Deposit _____

Due _____

Tumbler Order Form

Customer _____   Order N _____
Address _____   Order Date _____
Phone _____   Due Date _____
E-mail _____   Delivery By _____

Tumbler Details

Tumbler	Size	Quantity

Rush Order ☐ Yes   ☐ No

Decals

☐ Name   ☐ Monogram   ☐ Initials

Color _____
Font _____

☐ Quote   ☐ Text   ☐ Image

Color _____
Font _____

Design Details

Design Option	x	Color / Glitter Choices
Solid Color		
Ombre		
Full Glitter		
Half Glitter		

Note

Payment

☐ Cash   ☐ Venmo

☐ Check   ☐ Paypal

☐ Card   ☐ Other

Delivery

☐ Drop Off

☐ Pic Up

☐ Shipping

Pricing

Subtotal _____
Tax _____
Shipping _____
Grand total _____
Deposit _____
Due _____

Tumbler Order Form

Customer		Order N	
Address		Order Date	
Phone		Due Date	
E-mail		Delivery By	

Tumbler Details

Tumbler	Size	Quantity

Rush Order ☐ Yes ☐ No

Decals

☐ Name ☐ Monogram ☐ Initials

Color

Font

☐ Quote ☐ Text ☐ Image

Color

Font

Design Details

Design Option	x	Color / Glitter Choices
Solid Color		
Ombre		
Full Glitter		
Half Glitter		

Note

Payment

☐ Cash ☐ Venmo

☐ Check ☐ Paypal

☐ Card ☐ Other

Delivery

☐ Drop Off

☐ Pic Up

☐ Shipping

Pricing

Subtotal	
Tax	
Shipping	
Grand total	
Deposit	
Due	

Tumbler Order Form

Customer _____ Order N _____

Address _____ Order Date _____

Phone _____ Due Date _____

E-mail _____ Delivery By _____

Tumbler Details

Tumbler	Size	Quantity

Rush Order   ☐ Yes   ☐ No

Decals

☐ Name   ☐ Monogram   ☐ Initials

Color _____

Font _____

☐ Quote   ☐ Text   ☐ Image

Color _____

Font _____

Design Details

Design Option	x	Color / Glitter Choices
Solid Color		
Ombre		
Full Glitter		
Half Glitter		

Note

Payment

☐ Cash   ☐ Venmo

☐ Check   ☐ Paypal

☐ Card   ☐ Other

Delivery

☐ Drop Off

☐ Pic Up

☐ Shipping

Pricing

Subtotal _____

Tax _____

Shipping _____

Grand total _____

Deposit _____

Due _____

Tumbler Order Form

Customer _____ Order N _____
Address _____ Order Date _____
Phone _____ Due Date _____
E-mail _____ Delivery By _____

Tumbler Details

Tumbler	Size	Quantity

Rush Order ☐ Yes ☐ No

Decals

☐ Name ☐ Monogram ☐ Initials

Color _____
Font _____

☐ Quote ☐ Text ☐ Image

Color _____
Font _____

Design Details

Design Option	x	Color / Glitter Choices
Solid Color		
Ombre		
Full Glitter		
Half Glitter		

Note

Payment

☐ Cash ☐ Venmo
☐ Check ☐ Paypal
☐ Card ☐ Other

Delivery

☐ Drop Off
☐ Pic Up
☐ Shipping

Pricing

Subtotal _____
Tax _____
Shipping _____
Grand total _____
Deposit _____
Due _____

Tumbler Order Form

Customer	Order N
Address	Order Date
Phone	Due Date
E-mail	Delivery By

Tumbler Details

Tumbler	Size	Quantity

Rush Order ☐ Yes ☐ No

Decals

☐ Name ☐ Monogram ☐ Initials

Color _____

Font _____

☐ Quote ☐ Text ☐ Image

Color _____

Font _____

Design Details

Design Option	x	Color / Glitter Choices
Solid Color		
Ombre		
Full Glitter		
Half Glitter		

Note

Payment

☐ Cash ☐ Venmo

☐ Check ☐ Paypal

☐ Card ☐ Other

Delivery

☐ Drop Off

☐ Pic Up

☐ Shipping

Pricing

Subtotal	
Tax	
Shipping	
Grand total	
Deposit	
Due	

🥤 *Tumbler Order Form* 🥤

Customer		Order N
Address		Order Date
Phone		Due Date
E-mail		Delivery By

Tumbler Details

Tumbler	Size	Quantity

Rush Order   ☐ Yes   ☐ No

Decals

☐ Name   ☐ Monogram   ☐ Initials

Color

Font

☐ Quote   ☐ Text   ☐ Image

Color

Font

Design Details

Design Option	x	Color / Glitter Choices
Solid Color		
Ombre		
Full Glitter		
Half Glitter		

Note

Payment

☐ Cash	☐ Venmo
☐ Check	☐ Paypal
☐ Card	☐ Other

Delivery

☐ Drop Off

☐ Pic Up

☐ Shipping

Pricing

Subtotal	
Tax	
Shipping	
Grand total	
Deposit	
Due	

Tumbler Order Form

Customer _____   Order N _____
Address _____   Order Date _____
Phone _____   Due Date _____
E-mail _____   Delivery By _____

Tumbler Details

Tumbler	Size	Quantity

Rush Order   ☐ Yes   ☐ No

Decals

☐ Name   ☐ Monogram   ☐ Initials
_____

Color _____
Font _____

☐ Quote   ☐ Text   ☐ Image
_____

Color _____
Font _____

Design Details

Design Option	x	Color / Glitter Choices
Solid Color		
Ombre		
Full Glitter		
Half Glitter		

Note

Payment

☐ Cash   ☐ Venmo

☐ Check   ☐ Paypal

☐ Card   ☐ Other

Delivery

☐ Drop Off

☐ Pic Up

☐ Shipping

Pricing

Subtotal _____
Tax _____
Shipping _____
Grand total _____
Deposit _____
Due _____

Tumbler Order Form

Customer _____ Order N _____

Address _____ Order Date _____

Phone _____ Due Date _____

E-mail _____ Delivery By _____

Tumbler Details

Tumbler	Size	Quantity

Rush Order   ☐ Yes   ☐ No

Decals

☐ Name   ☐ Monogram   ☐ Initials

Color _____

Font _____

☐ Quote   ☐ Text   ☐ Image

Color _____

Font _____

Design Details

Design Option	x	Color / Glitter Choices
Solid Color		
Ombre		
Full Glitter		
Half Glitter		

Note

Payment

☐ Cash   ☐ Venmo

☐ Check   ☐ Paypal

☐ Card   ☐ Other

Delivery

☐ Drop Off

☐ Pic Up

☐ Shipping

Pricing

Subtotal _____

Tax _____

Shipping _____

Grand total _____

Deposit _____

Due _____

Tumbler Order Form

Customer		Order N	
Address		Order Date	
Phone		Due Date	
E-mail		Delivery By	

Tumbler Details

Tumbler	Size	Quantity

Rush Order ☐ Yes ☐ No

Decals

☐ Name ☐ Monogram ☐ Initials

Color

Font

☐ Quote ☐ Text ☐ Image

Color

Font

Design Details

Design Option	x	Color / Glitter Choices
Solid Color		
Ombre		
Full Glitter		
Half Glitter		

Note

Payment

☐ Cash ☐ Venmo

☐ Check ☐ Paypal

☐ Card ☐ Other

Delivery

☐ Drop Off

☐ Pic Up

☐ Shipping

Pricing

Subtotal

Tax

Shipping

Grand total

Deposit

Due

🥤 *Tumbler Order Form* 🥤

Customer _____   Order N _____

Address _____   Order Date _____

Phone _____   Due Date _____

E-mail _____   Delivery By _____

Tumbler Details

Tumbler	Size	Quantity

Rush Order   ☐ Yes   ☐ No

Decals

☐ Name   ☐ Monogram   ☐ Initials

Color _____

Font _____

☐ Quote   ☐ Text   ☐ Image

Color _____

Font _____

Design Details

Design Option	x	Color / Glitter Choices
Solid Color		
Ombre		
Full Glitter		
Half Glitter		

Note

Payment

☐ Cash   ☐ Venmo

☐ Check   ☐ Paypal

☐ Card   ☐ Other

Delivery

☐ Drop Off

☐ Pic Up

☐ Shipping

Pricing

Subtotal _____

Tax _____

Shipping _____

Grand total _____

Deposit _____

Due _____

Tumbler Order Form

Customer _____ Order N _____
Address _____ Order Date _____
Phone _____ Due Date _____
E-mail _____ Delivery By _____

Tumbler Details

Tumbler	Size	Quantity

Rush Order □ Yes □ No

Decals

□ Name □ Monogram □ Initials
_____
Color _____
Font _____
□ Quote □ Text □ Image
_____
Color _____
Font _____

Design Details

Design Option	x	Color / Glitter Choices
Solid Color		
Ombre		
Full Glitter		
Half Glitter		

Note

Payment

□ Cash □ Venmo
□ Check □ Paypal
□ Card □ Other

Delivery

□ Drop Off
□ Pic Up
□ Shipping

Pricing

Subtotal _____
Tax _____
Shipping _____
Grand total _____
Deposit _____
Due _____

Tumbler Order Form

Customer _____   Order N _____

Address _____   Order Date _____

Phone _____   Due Date _____

E-mail _____   Delivery By _____

Tumbler Details

Tumbler	Size	Quantity

Rush Order   ☐ Yes   ☐ No

Decals

☐ Name   ☐ Monogram   ☐ Initials

Color _____

Font _____

☐ Quote   ☐ Text   ☐ Image

Color _____

Font _____

Design Details

Design Option	x	Color / Glitter Choices
Solid Color		
Ombre		
Full Glitter		
Half Glitter		

Note

Payment

☐ Cash   ☐ Venmo

☐ Check   ☐ Paypal

☐ Card   ☐ Other

Delivery

☐ Drop Off

☐ Pic Up

☐ Shipping

Pricing

Subtotal _____

Tax _____

Shipping _____

Grand total _____

Deposit _____

Due _____

Tumbler Order Form

Customer		Order N	
Address		Order Date	
Phone		Due Date	
E-mail		Delivery By	

Tumbler Details

Tumbler	Size	Quantity

Rush Order   ☐ Yes   ☐ No

Decals

☐ Name   ☐ Monogram   ☐ Initials

Color _____

Font _____

☐ Quote   ☐ Text   ☐ Image

Color _____

Font _____

Design Details

Design Option	x	Color / Glitter Choices
Solid Color		
Ombre		
Full Glitter		
Half Glitter		

Note

Payment

☐ Cash	☐ Venmo	
☐ Check	☐ Paypal	
☐ Card	☐ Other	

Delivery

☐ Drop Off

☐ Pic Up

☐ Shipping

Pricing

Subtotal	
Tax	
Shipping	
Grand total	
Deposit	
Due	

Tumbler Order Form

Customer _____ Order N _____

Address _____ Order Date _____

Phone _____ Due Date _____

E-mail _____ Delivery By _____

Tumbler Details

Tumbler	Size	Quantity

Rush Order ☐ Yes ☐ No

Decals

☐ Name ☐ Monogram ☐ Initials

Color _____

Font _____

☐ Quote ☐ Text ☐ Image

Color _____

Font _____

Design Details

Design Option	x	Color / Glitter Choices
Solid Color		
Ombre		
Full Glitter		
Half Glitter		

Note

Payment

☐ Cash ☐ Venmo

☐ Check ☐ Paypal

☐ Card ☐ Other

Delivery

☐ Drop Off

☐ Pic Up

☐ Shipping

Pricing

Subtotal _____

Tax _____

Shipping _____

Grand total _____

Deposit _____

Due _____

Tumbler Order Form

Customer		Order N
Address		Order Date
Phone		Due Date
E-mail		Delivery By

Tumbler Details

Tumbler	Size	Quantity

Rush Order ☐ Yes ☐ No

Decals

☐ Name ☐ Monogram ☐ Initials

Color _____
Font _____

☐ Quote ☐ Text ☐ Image

Color _____
Font _____

Design Details

Design Option	x	Color / Glitter Choices
Solid Color		
Ombre		
Full Glitter		
Half Glitter		

Note

Payment

☐ Cash ☐ Venmo

☐ Check ☐ Paypal

☐ Card ☐ Other

Delivery

☐ Drop Off

☐ Pic Up

☐ Shipping

Pricing

Subtotal _____
Tax _____
Shipping _____
Grand total _____
Deposit _____
Due _____

Tumbler Order Form

Customer		Order N
Address		Order Date
Phone		Due Date
E-mail		Delivery By

Tumbler Details

Tumbler	Size	Quantity

Rush Order ☐ Yes ☐ No

Decals

☐ Name ☐ Monogram ☐ Initials

Color

Font

☐ Quote ☐ Text ☐ Image

Color

Font

Design Details

Design Option	x	Color / Glitter Choices
Solid Color		
Ombre		
Full Glitter		
Half Glitter		

Note

Payment

☐ Cash ☐ Venmo

☐ Check ☐ Paypal

☐ Card ☐ Other

Delivery

☐ Drop Off

☐ Pic Up

☐ Shipping

Pricing

Subtotal	
Tax	
Shipping	
Grand total	
Deposit	
Due	

Tumbler Order Form

Customer		Order N	
Address		Order Date	
Phone		Due Date	
E-mail		Delivery By	

Tumbler Details

Tumbler	Size	Quantity

Rush Order   ☐ Yes   ☐ No

Decals

☐ Name   ☐ Monogram   ☐ Initials

Color _____

Font _____

☐ Quote   ☐ Text   ☐ Image

Color _____

Font _____

Design Details

Design Option	x	Color / Glitter Choices
Solid Color		
Ombre		
Full Glitter		
Half Glitter		

Note

Payment

☐ Cash	☐ Venmo
☐ Check	☐ Paypal
☐ Card	☐ Other

Delivery

☐ Drop Off

☐ Pic Up

☐ Shipping

Pricing

Subtotal	
Tax	
Shipping	
Grand total	
Deposit	
Due	

Tumbler Order Form

Customer _____   Order N _____
Address _____   Order Date _____
Phone _____   Due Date _____
E-mail _____   Delivery By _____

Tumbler Details

Tumbler	Size	Quantity

Rush Order   □ Yes   □ No

Decals

□ Name   □ Monogram   □ Initials

Color _____
Font _____

□ Quote   □ Text   □ Image

Color _____
Font _____

Design Details

Design Option	x	Color / Glitter Choices
Solid Color		
Ombre		
Full Glitter		
Half Glitter		

Note

Payment

□ Cash   □ Venmo

□ Check   □ Paypal

□ Card   □ Other

Delivery

□ Drop Off

□ Pic Up

□ Shipping

Pricing

Subtotal _____
Tax _____
Shipping _____
Grand total _____
Deposit _____
Due _____

Tumbler Order Form

Customer _____ Order N _____
Address _____ Order Date _____
Phone _____ Due Date _____
E-mail _____ Delivery By _____

Tumbler Details

Tumbler	Size	Quantity

Rush Order   ☐ Yes   ☐ No

Decals

☐ Name   ☐ Monogram   ☐ Initials

Color _____
Font _____

☐ Quote   ☐ Text   ☐ Image

Color _____
Font _____

Design Details

Design Option	x	Color / Glitter Choices
Solid Color		
Ombre		
Full Glitter		
Half Glitter		

Note

Payment

☐ Cash   ☐ Venmo

☐ Check   ☐ Paypal

☐ Card   ☐ Other

Delivery

☐ Drop Off

☐ Pic Up

☐ Shipping

Pricing

Subtotal _____
Tax _____
Shipping _____
Grand total _____
Deposit _____
Due _____

Tumbler Order Form

Customer _____   Order N _____

Address _____   Order Date _____

Phone _____   Due Date _____

E-mail _____   Delivery By _____

Tumbler Details

Tumbler	Size	Quantity

Rush Order   ☐ Yes   ☐ No

Decals

☐ Name   ☐ Monogram   ☐ Initials

Color _____

Font _____

☐ Quote   ☐ Text   ☐ Image

Color _____

Font _____

Design Details

Design Option	x	Color / Glitter Choices
Solid Color		
Ombre		
Full Glitter		
Half Glitter		

Note

Payment

☐ Cash   ☐ Venmo

☐ Check   ☐ Paypal

☐ Card   ☐ Other

Delivery

☐ Drop Off

☐ Pic Up

☐ Shipping

Pricing

Subtotal _____

Tax _____

Shipping _____

Grand total _____

Deposit _____

Due _____

Tumbler Order Form

Customer _____ Order N _____

Address _____ Order Date _____

Phone _____ Due Date _____

E-mail _____ Delivery By _____

Tumbler Details

Tumbler	Size	Quantity

Rush Order   ☐ Yes   ☐ No

Decals

☐ Name   ☐ Monogram   ☐ Initials

Color _____

Font _____

☐ Quote   ☐ Text   ☐ Image

Color _____

Font _____

Design Details

Design Option	x	Color / Glitter Choices
Solid Color		
Ombre		
Full Glitter		
Half Glitter		

Note

Payment

☐ Cash   ☐ Venmo

☐ Check   ☐ Paypal

☐ Card   ☐ Other

Delivery

☐ Drop Off

☐ Pic Up

☐ Shipping

Pricing

Subtotal _____

Tax _____

Shipping _____

Grand total _____

Deposit _____

Due _____

Tumbler Order Form

Customer		Order N
Address		Order Date
Phone		Due Date
E-mail		Delivery By

Tumbler Details

Tumbler	Size	Quantity

Rush Order □ Yes □ No

Decals

□ Name □ Monogram □ Initials

Color

Font

□ Quote □ Text □ Image

Color

Font

Design Details

Design Option	x	Color / Glitter Choices
Solid Color		
Ombre		
Full Glitter		
Half Glitter		

Note

Payment

□ Cash □ Venmo

□ Check □ Paypal

□ Card □ Other

Delivery

□ Drop Off

□ Pic Up

□ Shipping

Pricing

Subtotal

Tax

Shipping

Grand total

Deposit

Due

Tumbler Order Form

Customer		Order N	
Address		Order Date	
Phone		Due Date	
E-mail		Delivery By	

Tumbler Details

Tumbler	Size	Quantity

Rush Order   ☐ Yes   ☐ No

Decals

☐ Name   ☐ Monogram   ☐ Initials

Color

Font

☐ Quote   ☐ Text   ☐ Image

Color

Font

Design Details

Design Option	x	Color / Glitter Choices
Solid Color		
Ombre		
Full Glitter		
Half Glitter		

Note

Payment

☐ Cash   ☐ Venmo

☐ Check   ☐ Paypal

☐ Card   ☐ Other

Delivery

☐ Drop Off

☐ Pic Up

☐ Shipping

Pricing

Subtotal

Tax

Shipping

Grand total

Deposit

Due

Tumbler Order Form

Customer _____   Order N _____
Address _____   Order Date _____
Phone _____   Due Date _____
E-mail _____   Delivery By _____

Tumbler Details

Tumbler	Size	Quantity

Rush Order ☐ Yes   ☐ No

Decals

☐ Name   ☐ Monogram   ☐ Initials

Color _____
Font _____

☐ Quote   ☐ Text   ☐ Image

Color _____
Font _____

Design Details

Design Option	x	Color / Glitter Choices
Solid Color		
Ombre		
Full Glitter		
Half Glitter		

Note

Payment

☐ Cash   ☐ Venmo

☐ Check   ☐ Paypal

☐ Card   ☐ Other

Delivery

☐ Drop Off

☐ Pic Up

☐ Shipping

Pricing

Subtotal _____
Tax _____
Shipping _____
Grand total _____
Deposit _____
Due _____

🥤 *Tumbler Order Form* 🥤

Customer		Order N
Address		Order Date
Phone		Due Date
E-mail		Delivery By

Tumbler Details

Tumbler	Size	Quantity

Rush Order   ☐ Yes   ☐ No

Decals

☐ Name   ☐ Monogram   ☐ Initials

Color _____
Font _____

☐ Quote   ☐ Text   ☐ Image

Color _____
Font _____

Design Details

Design Option	x	Color / Glitter Choices
Solid Color		
Ombre		
Full Glitter		
Half Glitter		

Note

Payment

☐ Cash	☐ Venmo
☐ Check	☐ Paypal
☐ Card	☐ Other

Delivery

☐ Drop Off

☐ Pic Up

☐ Shipping

Pricing

Subtotal _____
Tax _____
Shipping _____
Grand total _____
Deposit _____
Due _____

Tumbler Order Form

Customer _____ Order N _____

Address _____ Order Date _____

Phone _____ Due Date _____

E-mail _____ Delivery By _____

Tumbler Details

Tumbler	Size	Quantity

Rush Order   □ Yes   □ No

Decals

□ Name   □ Monogram   □ Initials

Color _____

Font _____

□ Quote   □ Text   □ Image

Color _____

Font _____

Design Details

Design Option	x	Color / Glitter Choices
Solid Color		
Ombre		
Full Glitter		
Half Glitter		

Note

Payment

□ Cash   □ Venmo

□ Check   □ Paypal

□ Card   □ Other

Delivery

□ Drop Off

□ Pic Up

□ Shipping

Pricing

Subtotal _____

Tax _____

Shipping _____

Grand total _____

Deposit _____

Due _____

Tumbler Order Form

Customer _____ Order N _____

Address _____ Order Date _____

Phone _____ Due Date _____

E-mail _____ Delivery By _____

Tumbler Details

Tumbler	Size	Quantity

Rush Order   ☐ Yes   ☐ No

Decals

☐ Name   ☐ Monogram   ☐ Initials

_____

Color _____

Font _____

☐ Quote   ☐ Text   ☐ Image

_____

Color _____

Font _____

Design Details

Design Option	x	Color / Glitter Choices
Solid Color		
Ombre		
Full Glitter		
Half Glitter		

Note

_____

_____

_____

_____

_____

Payment

☐ Cash   ☐ Venmo

☐ Check   ☐ Paypal

☐ Card   ☐ Other

Delivery

☐ Drop Off

☐ Pic Up

☐ Shipping

Pricing

Subtotal _____

Tax _____

Shipping _____

Grand total _____

Deposit _____

Due _____

Tumbler Order Form

Customer _____ Order N _____

Address _____ Order Date _____

Phone _____ Due Date _____

E-mail _____ Delivery By _____

Tumbler Details

Tumbler	Size	Quantity

Rush Order   □ Yes   □ No

Decals

□ Name   □ Monogram   □ Initials

Color _____

Font _____

□ Quote   □ Text   □ Image

Color _____

Font _____

Design Details

Design Option	x	Color / Glitter Choices
Solid Color		
Ombre		
Full Glitter		
Half Glitter		

Note

Payment

□ Cash   □ Venmo

□ Check   □ Paypal

□ Card   □ Other

Delivery

□ Drop Off

□ Pic Up

□ Shipping

Pricing

Subtotal _____

Tax _____

Shipping _____

Grand total _____

Deposit _____

Due _____

Tumbler Order Form

Customer		Order N	
Address		Order Date	
Phone		Due Date	
E-mail		Delivery By	

Tumbler Details

Tumbler	Size	Quantity

Rush Order   ☐ Yes   ☐ No

Decals

☐ Name   ☐ Monogram   ☐ Initials

Color _____

Font _____

☐ Quote   ☐ Text   ☐ Image

Color _____

Font _____

Design Details

Design Option	x	Color / Glitter Choices
Solid Color		
Ombre		
Full Glitter		
Half Glitter		

Note

Payment

☐ Cash	☐ Venmo
☐ Check	☐ Paypal
☐ Card	☐ Other

Delivery

☐ Drop Off

☐ Pic Up

☐ Shipping

Pricing

Subtotal _____

Tax _____

Shipping _____

Grand total _____

Deposit _____

Due _____

Tumbler Order Form

Customer _____ Order N _____

Address _____ Order Date _____

Phone _____ Due Date _____

E-mail _____ Delivery By _____

Tumbler Details

Tumbler	Size	Quantity

Rush Order ☐ Yes ☐ No

Decals

☐ Name ☐ Monogram ☐ Initials

Color _____

Font _____

☐ Quote ☐ Text ☐ Image

Color _____

Font _____

Design Details

Design Option	x	Color / Glitter Choices
Solid Color		
Ombre		
Full Glitter		
Half Glitter		

Note

Payment

☐ Cash ☐ Venmo

☐ Check ☐ Paypal

☐ Card ☐ Other

Delivery

☐ Drop Off

☐ Pic Up

☐ Shipping

Pricing

Subtotal _____

Tax _____

Shipping _____

Grand total _____

Deposit _____

Due _____

Tumbler Order Form

Customer _____ Order N _____
Address _____ Order Date _____
Phone _____ Due Date _____
E-mail _____ Delivery By _____

Tumbler Details

Tumbler	Size	Quantity

Rush Order   □ Yes   □ No

Decals

□ Name   □ Monogram   □ Initials

Color _____
Font _____

□ Quote   □ Text   □ Image

Color _____
Font _____

Design Details

Design Option	x	Color / Glitter Choices
Solid Color		
Ombre		
Full Glitter		
Half Glitter		

Note

Payment

□ Cash   □ Venmo
□ Check   □ Paypal
□ Card   □ Other

Delivery

□ Drop Off
□ Pic Up
□ Shipping

Pricing

Subtotal _____
Tax _____
Shipping _____
Grand total _____
Deposit _____
Due _____

Tumbler Order Form

Customer ....   Order N ....

Address ....   Order Date ....

Phone ....   Due Date ....

E-mail ....   Delivery By ....

Tumbler Details

Tumbler	Size	Quantity

Rush Order   ☐ Yes   ☐ No

Decals

☐ Name   ☐ Monogram   ☐ Initials

Color ....

Font ....

☐ Quote   ☐ Text   ☐ Image

Color ....

Font ....

Design Details

Design Option	x	Color / Glitter Choices
Solid Color		
Ombre		
Full Glitter		
Half Glitter		

Note

Payment

☐ Cash   ☐ Venmo

☐ Check   ☐ Paypal

☐ Card   ☐ Other

Delivery

☐ Drop Off

☐ Pic Up

☐ Shipping

Pricing

Subtotal ....

Tax ....

Shipping ....

Grand total ....

Deposit ....

Due ....

Tumbler Order Form

Customer _____ Order N _____

Address _____ Order Date _____

Phone _____ Due Date _____

E-mail _____ Delivery By _____

Tumbler Details

Tumbler	Size	Quantity

Rush Order   ☐ Yes   ☐ No

Decals

☐ Name   ☐ Monogram   ☐ Initials

Color _____

Font _____

☐ Quote   ☐ Text   ☐ Image

Color _____

Font _____

Design Details

Design Option	x	Color / Glitter Choices
Solid Color		
Ombre		
Full Glitter		
Half Glitter		

Note

Payment

☐ Cash   ☐ Venmo

☐ Check   ☐ Paypal

☐ Card   ☐ Other

Delivery

☐ Drop Off

☐ Pic Up

☐ Shipping

Pricing

Subtotal _____

Tax _____

Shipping _____

Grand total _____

Deposit _____

Due _____

Tumbler Order Form

Customer _____ Order N _____
Address _____ Order Date _____
Phone _____ Due Date _____
E-mail _____ Delivery By _____

Tumbler Details

Tumbler	Size	Quantity

Rush Order ☐ Yes   ☐ No

Decals

☐ Name   ☐ Monogram   ☐ Initials

Color _____
Font _____

☐ Quote   ☐ Text   ☐ Image

Color _____
Font _____

Design Details

Design Option	x	Color / Glitter Choices
Solid Color		
Ombre		
Full Glitter		
Half Glitter		

Note

Payment

☐ Cash   ☐ Venmo

☐ Check   ☐ Paypal

☐ Card   ☐ Other

Delivery

☐ Drop Off

☐ Pic Up

☐ Shipping

Pricing

Subtotal _____
Tax _____
Shipping _____
Grand total _____
Deposit _____
Due _____

🥤 Tumbler Order Form 🥤

Customer _____	Order N _____
Address _____	Order Date _____
Phone _____	Due Date _____
E-mail _____	Delivery By _____

Tumbler Details

Tumbler	Size	Quantity

Rush Order ☐ Yes   ☐ No

Decals

☐ Name   ☐ Monogram   ☐ Initials

Color _____

Font _____

☐ Quote   ☐ Text   ☐ Image

Color _____

Font _____

Design Details

Design Option	x	Color / Glitter Choices
Solid Color		
Ombre		
Full Glitter		
Half Glitter		

Note

Payment

☐ Cash	☐ Venmo
☐ Check	☐ Paypal
☐ Card	☐ Other

Delivery

☐ Drop Off

☐ Pic Up

☐ Shipping

Pricing

Subtotal	_____
Tax	_____
Shipping	_____
Grand total	_____
Deposit	_____
Due	_____

Tumbler Order Form

Customer _____ Order N _____
Address _____ Order Date _____
Phone _____ Due Date _____
E-mail _____ Delivery By _____

Tumbler Details

Tumbler	Size	Quantity

Rush Order □ Yes □ No

Decals

□ Name □ Monogram □ Initials

Color _____
Font _____

□ Quote □ Text □ Image

Color _____
Font _____

Design Details

Design Option	x	Color / Glitter Choices
Solid Color		
Ombre		
Full Glitter		
Half Glitter		

Note

Payment

□ Cash □ Venmo

□ Check □ Paypal

□ Card □ Other

Delivery

□ Drop Off

□ Pic Up

□ Shipping

Pricing

Subtotal _____
Tax _____
Shipping _____
Grand total _____
Deposit _____
Due _____

Tumbler Order Form

Customer _____   Order N _____
Address _____   Order Date _____
Phone _____   Due Date _____
E-mail _____   Delivery By _____

Tumbler Details

Tumbler	Size	Quantity

Rush Order   ☐ Yes   ☐ No

Decals

☐ Name   ☐ Monogram   ☐ Initials

Color _____
Font _____

☐ Quote   ☐ Text   ☐ Image

Color _____
Font _____

Design Details

Design Option	x	Color / Glitter Choices
Solid Color		
Ombre		
Full Glitter		
Half Glitter		

Note

Payment

☐ Cash   ☐ Venmo

☐ Check   ☐ Paypal

☐ Card   ☐ Other

Delivery

☐ Drop Off

☐ Pic Up

☐ Shipping

Pricing

Subtotal _____
Tax _____
Shipping _____
Grand total _____
Deposit _____
Due _____

Tumbler Order Form

Customer	Order N
Address	Order Date
Phone	Due Date
E-mail	Delivery By

Tumbler Details

Tumbler	Size	Quantity

Rush Order   □ Yes   □ No

Decals

□ Name   □ Monogram   □ Initials

Color

Font

□ Quote   □ Text   □ Image

Color

Font

Design Details

Design Option	x	Color / Glitter Choices
Solid Color		
Ombre		
Full Glitter		
Half Glitter		

Note

Payment

□ Cash	□ Venmo	
□ Check	□ Paypal	
□ Card	□ Other	

Delivery

□ Drop Off

□ Pic Up

□ Shipping

Pricing

Subtotal	
Tax	
Shipping	
Grand total	
Deposit	
Due	

Tumbler Order Form

Customer .... Order N ....
Address .... Order Date ....
Phone .... Due Date ....
E-mail .... Delivery By ....

Tumbler Details

Tumbler	Size	Quantity

Rush Order   ☐ Yes   ☐ No

Decals

☐ Name   ☐ Monogram   ☐ Initials

Color ....
Font ....

☐ Quote   ☐ Text   ☐ Image

Color ....
Font ....

Design Details

Design Option	x	Color / Glitter Choices
Solid Color		
Ombre		
Full Glitter		
Half Glitter		

Note

Payment

☐ Cash   ☐ Venmo

☐ Check   ☐ Paypal

☐ Card   ☐ Other

Delivery

☐ Drop Off

☐ Pic Up

☐ Shipping

Pricing

Subtotal ....
Tax ....
Shipping ....
Grand total ....
Deposit ....
Due ....

Tumbler Order Form

Customer		Order N
Address		Order Date
Phone		Due Date
E-mail		Delivery By

Tumbler Details

Tumbler	Size	Quantity

Rush Order   ☐ Yes   ☐ No

Decals

☐ Name   ☐ Monogram   ☐ Initials

Color

Font

☐ Quote   ☐ Text   ☐ Image

Color

Font

Design Details

Design Option	x	Color / Glitter Choices
Solid Color		
Ombre		
Full Glitter		
Half Glitter		

Note

Payment

☐ Cash	☐ Venmo
☐ Check	☐ Paypal
☐ Card	☐ Other

Delivery

☐ Drop Off

☐ Pic Up

☐ Shipping

Pricing

Subtotal

Tax

Shipping

Grand total

Deposit

Due

Tumbler Order Form

Customer _____   Order N _____

Address _____   Order Date _____

Phone _____   Due Date _____

E-mail _____   Delivery By _____

Tumbler Details

Tumbler	Size	Quantity

Rush Order   ☐ Yes   ☐ No

Decals

☐ Name   ☐ Monogram   ☐ Initials

Color _____

Font _____

☐ Quote   ☐ Text   ☐ Image

Color _____

Font _____

Design Details

Design Option	x	Color / Glitter Choices
Solid Color		
Ombre		
Full Glitter		
Half Glitter		

Note

Payment

☐ Cash   ☐ Venmo

☐ Check   ☐ Paypal

☐ Card   ☐ Other

Delivery

☐ Drop Off

☐ Pic Up

☐ Shipping

Pricing

Subtotal _____

Tax _____

Shipping _____

Grand total _____

Deposit _____

Due _____

Tumbler Order Form

Customer _____ Order N _____

Address _____ Order Date _____

Phone _____ Due Date _____

E-mail _____ Delivery By _____

Tumbler Details

Tumbler	Size	Quantity

Rush Order   ☐ Yes   ☐ No

Decals

☐ Name   ☐ Monogram   ☐ Initials

Color _____

Font _____

☐ Quote   ☐ Text   ☐ Image

Color _____

Font _____

Design Details

Design Option	x	Color / Glitter Choices
Solid Color		
Ombre		
Full Glitter		
Half Glitter		

Note

Payment

☐ Cash   ☐ Venmo

☐ Check   ☐ Paypal

☐ Card   ☐ Other

Delivery

☐ Drop Off

☐ Pic Up

☐ Shipping

Pricing

Subtotal _____

Tax _____

Shipping _____

Grand total _____

Deposit _____

Due _____

Tumbler Order Form

Customer _____ Order N _____

Address _____ Order Date _____

Phone _____ Due Date _____

E-mail _____ Delivery By _____

Tumbler Details

Tumbler	Size	Quantity

Rush Order   □ Yes   □ No

Decals

□ Name   □ Monogram   □ Initials

Color _____

Font _____

□ Quote   □ Text   □ Image

Color _____

Font _____

Design Details

Design Option	x	Color / Glitter Choices
Solid Color		
Ombre		
Full Glitter		
Half Glitter		

Note

Payment

□ Cash   □ Venmo

□ Check   □ Paypal

□ Card   □ Other

Delivery

□ Drop Off

□ Pic Up

□ Shipping

Pricing

Subtotal _____

Tax _____

Shipping _____

Grand total _____

Deposit _____

Due _____

Tumbler Order Form

Customer _____   Order N _____

Address _____   Order Date _____

Phone _____   Due Date _____

E-mail _____   Delivery By _____

Tumbler Details

Tumbler	Size	Quantity

Rush Order   ☐ Yes   ☐ No

Decals

☐ Name   ☐ Monogram   ☐ Initials

Color _____

Font _____

☐ Quote   ☐ Text   ☐ Image

Color _____

Font _____

Design Details

Design Option	x	Color / Glitter Choices
Solid Color		
Ombre		
Full Glitter		
Half Glitter		

Note

Payment

☐ Cash   ☐ Venmo

☐ Check   ☐ Paypal

☐ Card   ☐ Other

Delivery

☐ Drop Off

☐ Pic Up

☐ Shipping

Pricing

Subtotal _____

Tax _____

Shipping _____

Grand total _____

Deposit _____

Due _____

🥤 Tumbler Order Form 🥤

Customer _____   Order N _____
Address _____   Order Date _____
Phone _____   Due Date _____
E-mail _____   Delivery By _____

Tumbler Details

Tumbler	Size	Quantity

Rush Order   □ Yes   □ No

Decals

□ Name   □ Monogram   □ Initials
_____
Color _____
Font _____

□ Quote   □ Text   □ Image
_____
Color _____
Font _____

Design Details

Design Option	x	Color / Glitter Choices
Solid Color		
Ombre		
Full Glitter		
Half Glitter		

Note

Payment

□ Cash   □ Venmo

□ Check   □ Paypal

□ Card   □ Other

Delivery

□ Drop Off

□ Pic Up

□ Shipping

Pricing

Subtotal _____
Tax _____
Shipping _____
Grand total _____
Deposit _____
Due _____

Tumbler Order Form

Customer _____ Order N _____
Address _____ Order Date _____
Phone _____ Due Date _____
E-mail _____ Delivery By _____

Tumbler Details

Tumbler	Size	Quantity

Rush Order   ☐ Yes   ☐ No

Decals

☐ Name   ☐ Monogram   ☐ Initials

Color _____
Font _____

☐ Quote   ☐ Text   ☐ Image

Color _____
Font _____

Design Details

Design Option	x	Color / Glitter Choices
Solid Color		
Ombre		
Full Glitter		
Half Glitter		

Note

Payment

☐ Cash   ☐ Venmo
☐ Check   ☐ Paypal
☐ Card   ☐ Other

Delivery

☐ Drop Off
☐ Pic Up
☐ Shipping

Pricing

Subtotal _____
Tax _____
Shipping _____
Grand total _____
Deposit _____
Due _____

Tumbler Order Form

Customer ....

Address ....

Phone ....

E-mail ....

Order N ....

Order Date ....

Due Date ....

Delivery By ....

Tumbler Details

Tumbler	Size	Quantity

Rush Order   ☐ Yes   ☐ No

Decals

☐ Name   ☐ Monogram   ☐ Initials

Color ....

Font ....

☐ Quote   ☐ Text   ☐ Image

Color ....

Font ....

Design Details

Design Option	x	Color / Glitter Choices
Solid Color		
Ombre		
Full Glitter		
Half Glitter		

Note

Payment

☐ Cash   ☐ Venmo

☐ Check   ☐ Paypal

☐ Card   ☐ Other

Delivery

☐ Drop Off

☐ Pic Up

☐ Shipping

Pricing

Subtotal ....

Tax ....

Shipping ....

Grand total ....

Deposit ....

Due ....

Tumbler Order Form

Customer	Order N
Address	Order Date
Phone	Due Date
E-mail	Delivery By

Tumbler Details

Tumbler	Size	Quantity

Rush Order ☐ Yes ☐ No

Decals

☐ Name ☐ Monogram ☐ Initials

Color

Font

☐ Quote ☐ Text ☐ Image

Color

Font

Design Details

Design Option	x	Color / Glitter Choices
Solid Color		
Ombre		
Full Glitter		
Half Glitter		

Note

Payment

☐ Cash ☐ Venmo

☐ Check ☐ Paypal

☐ Card ☐ Other

Delivery

☐ Drop Off

☐ Pic Up

☐ Shipping

Pricing

Subtotal	
Tax	
Shipping	
Grand total	
Deposit	
Due	

🥤 Tumbler Order Form 🥤

Customer _____   Order N _____
Address _____   Order Date _____
Phone _____   Due Date _____
E-mail _____   Delivery By _____

Tumbler Details

Tumbler	Size	Quantity

Rush Order   ☐ Yes   ☐ No

Decals

☐ Name   ☐ Monogram   ☐ Initials

Color _____
Font _____

☐ Quote   ☐ Text   ☐ Image

Color _____
Font _____

Design Details

Design Option	x	Color / Glitter Choices
Solid Color		
Ombre		
Full Glitter		
Half Glitter		

Note

Payment

☐ Cash   ☐ Venmo
☐ Check   ☐ Paypal
☐ Card   ☐ Other

Delivery

☐ Drop Off
☐ Pic Up
☐ Shipping

Pricing

Subtotal _____
Tax _____
Shipping _____
Grand total _____
Deposit _____
Due _____

🥤 *Tumbler Order Form* 🥤

Customer		Order N
Address		Order Date
Phone		Due Date
E-mail		Delivery By

Tumbler Details

Tumbler	Size	Quantity

Rush Order   ☐ Yes   ☐ No

Decals

☐ Name   ☐ Monogram   ☐ Initials

Color

Font

☐ Quote   ☐ Text   ☐ Image

Color

Font

Design Details

Design Option	x	Color / Glitter Choices
Solid Color		
Ombre		
Full Glitter		
Half Glitter		

Note

Payment

☐ Cash	☐ Venmo	
☐ Check	☐ Paypal	
☐ Card	☐ Other	

Delivery

☐ Drop Off

☐ Pic Up

☐ Shipping

Pricing

Subtotal

Tax

Shipping

Grand total

Deposit

Due

Tumbler Order Form

Customer _____ Order N _____

Address _____ Order Date _____

Phone _____ Due Date _____

E-mail _____ Delivery By _____

Tumbler Details

Tumbler	Size	Quantity

Rush Order   ☐ Yes   ☐ No

Decals

☐ Name   ☐ Monogram   ☐ Initials

Color _____

Font _____

☐ Quote   ☐ Text   ☐ Image

Color _____

Font _____

Design Details

Design Option	x	Color / Glitter Choices
Solid Color		
Ombre		
Full Glitter		
Half Glitter		

Note

Payment

☐ Cash   ☐ Venmo

☐ Check   ☐ Paypal

☐ Card   ☐ Other

Delivery

☐ Drop Off

☐ Pic Up

☐ Shipping

Pricing

Subtotal _____

Tax _____

Shipping _____

Grand total _____

Deposit _____

Due _____

Tumbler Order Form

Customer _____ Order N _____
Address _____ Order Date _____
Phone _____ Due Date _____
E-mail _____ Delivery By _____

Tumbler Details

Tumbler	Size	Quantity

Rush Order ☐ Yes   ☐ No

Decals

☐ Name ☐ Monogram ☐ Initials

Color _____
Font _____

☐ Quote   ☐ Text   ☐ Image

Color _____
Font _____

Design Details

Design Option	x	Color / Glitter Choices
Solid Color		
Ombre		
Full Glitter		
Half Glitter		

Note

Payment

☐ Cash   ☐ Venmo

☐ Check   ☐ Paypal

☐ Card   ☐ Other

Delivery

☐ Drop Off

☐ Pic Up

☐ Shipping

Pricing

Subtotal _____
Tax _____
Shipping _____
Grand total _____
Deposit _____
Due _____

🥤 Tumbler Order Form 🥤

Customer _____   Order N _____
Address _____   Order Date _____
Phone _____   Due Date _____
E-mail _____   Delivery By _____

Tumbler Details

Tumbler	Size	Quantity

Rush Order   ☐ Yes   ☐ No

Decals

☐ Name   ☐ Monogram   ☐ Initials

Color _____
Font _____

☐ Quote   ☐ Text   ☐ Image

Color _____
Font _____

Design Details

Design Option	x	Color / Glitter Choices
Solid Color		
Ombre		
Full Glitter		
Half Glitter		

Note

_____
_____
_____
_____
_____
_____

Payment

☐ Cash   ☐ Venmo
☐ Check   ☐ Paypal
☐ Card   ☐ Other

Delivery

☐ Drop Off
☐ Pic Up
☐ Shipping

Pricing

Subtotal _____
Tax _____
Shipping _____
Grand total _____
Deposit _____
Due _____

Tumbler Order Form

Customer _____   Order N _____
Address _____   Order Date _____
Phone _____   Due Date _____
E-mail _____   Delivery By _____

Tumbler Details

Tumbler	Size	Quantity

Rush Order   ☐ Yes   ☐ No

Decals

☐ Name   ☐ Monogram   ☐ Initials

Color _____
Font _____

☐ Quote   ☐ Text   ☐ Image

Color _____
Font _____

Design Details

Design Option	x	Color / Glitter Choices
Solid Color		
Ombre		
Full Glitter		
Half Glitter		

Note

Payment

☐ Cash   ☐ Venmo
☐ Check   ☐ Paypal
☐ Card   ☐ Other

Delivery

☐ Drop Off
☐ Pic Up
☐ Shipping

Pricing

Subtotal _____
Tax _____
Shipping _____
Grand total _____
Deposit _____
Due _____

Tumbler Order Form

Customer _____ Order N _____

Address _____ Order Date _____

Phone _____ Due Date _____

E-mail _____ Delivery By _____

Tumbler Details

Tumbler	Size	Quantity

Rush Order ☐ Yes   ☐ No

Decals

☐ Name ☐ Monogram ☐ Initials

Color _____

Font _____

☐ Quote   ☐ Text   ☐ Image

Color _____

Font _____

Design Details

Design Option	x	Color / Glitter Choices
Solid Color		
Ombre		
Full Glitter		
Half Glitter		

Note

Payment

☐ Cash   ☐ Venmo

☐ Check   ☐ Paypal

☐ Card   ☐ Other

Delivery

☐ Drop Off

☐ Pic Up

☐ Shipping

Pricing

Subtotal _____

Tax _____

Shipping _____

Grand total _____

Deposit _____

Due _____

Tumbler Order Form

Customer _____ Order N _____

Address _____ Order Date _____

Phone _____ Due Date _____

E-mail _____ Delivery By _____

Tumbler Details

Tumbler	Size	Quantity

Rush Order   ☐ Yes   ☐ No

Decals

☐ Name   ☐ Monogram   ☐ Initials

Color _____

Font _____

☐ Quote   ☐ Text   ☐ Image

Color _____

Font _____

Design Details

Design Option	x	Color / Glitter Choices
Solid Color		
Ombre		
Full Glitter		
Half Glitter		

Note

Payment

☐ Cash   ☐ Venmo

☐ Check   ☐ Paypal

☐ Card   ☐ Other

Delivery

☐ Drop Off

☐ Pic Up

☐ Shipping

Pricing

Subtotal _____

Tax _____

Shipping _____

Grand total _____

Deposit _____

Due _____

Tumbler Order Form

Customer		Order N	
Address		Order Date	
Phone		Due Date	
E-mail		Delivery By	

Tumbler Details

Tumbler	Size	Quantity

Rush Order □ Yes   □ No

Decals

□ Name □ Monogram □ Initials

Color _____

Font _____

□ Quote   □ Text   □ Image

Color _____

Font _____

Design Details

Design Option	x	Color / Glitter Choices
Solid Color		
Ombre		
Full Glitter		
Half Glitter		

Note

Payment

□ Cash	□ Venmo
□ Check	□ Paypal
□ Card	□ Other

Delivery

□ Drop Off

□ Pic Up

□ Shipping

Pricing

Subtotal	
Tax	
Shipping	
Grand total	
Deposit	
Due	

Tumbler Order Form

Customer		Order N
Address		Order Date
Phone		Due Date
E-mail		Delivery By

Tumbler Details

Tumbler	Size	Quantity

Rush Order ☐ Yes   ☐ No

Decals

☐ Name ☐ Monogram ☐ Initials

Color _____

Font _____

☐ Quote   ☐ Text   ☐ Image

Color _____

Font _____

Design Details

Design Option	x	Color / Glitter Choices
Solid Color		
Ombre		
Full Glitter		
Half Glitter		

Note

Payment

☐ Cash   ☐ Venmo

☐ Check   ☐ Paypal

☐ Card   ☐ Other

Delivery

☐ Drop Off

☐ Pic Up

☐ Shipping

Pricing

Subtotal _____

Tax _____

Shipping _____

Grand total _____

Deposit _____

Due _____

Tumbler Order Form

Customer ....   Order N ....

Address ....   Order Date ....

Phone ....   Due Date ....

E-mail ....   Delivery By ....

Tumbler Details

Tumbler	Size	Quantity

Rush Order   ☐ Yes   ☐ No

Decals

☐ Name   ☐ Monogram   ☐ Initials

Color ....

Font ....

☐ Quote   ☐ Text   ☐ Image

Color ....

Font ....

Design Details

Design Option	x	Color / Glitter Choices
Solid Color		
Ombre		
Full Glitter		
Half Glitter		

Note

Payment

☐ Cash   ☐ Venmo

☐ Check   ☐ Paypal

☐ Card   ☐ Other

Delivery

☐ Drop Off

☐ Pic Up

☐ Shipping

Pricing

Subtotal ....

Tax ....

Shipping ....

Grand total ....

Deposit ....

Due ....

Tumbler Order Form

Customer _____ Order N _____

Address _____ Order Date _____

Phone _____ Due Date _____

E-mail _____ Delivery By _____

Tumbler Details

Tumbler	Size	Quantity

Rush Order   ☐ Yes   ☐ No

Decals

☐ Name   ☐ Monogram   ☐ Initials

Color _____

Font _____

☐ Quote   ☐ Text   ☐ Image

Color _____

Font _____

Design Details

Design Option	x	Color / Glitter Choices
Solid Color		
Ombre		
Full Glitter		
Half Glitter		

Note

Payment

☐ Cash   ☐ Venmo

☐ Check   ☐ Paypal

☐ Card   ☐ Other

Delivery

☐ Drop Off

☐ Pic Up

☐ Shipping

Pricing

Subtotal _____

Tax _____

Shipping _____

Grand total _____

Deposit _____

Due _____

🥤 *Tumbler Order Form* 🥤

Customer _____	Order N _____
Address _____	Order Date _____
Phone _____	Due Date _____
E-mail _____	Delivery By _____

Tumbler Details

Tumbler	Size	Quantity

Rush Order   ☐ Yes   ☐ No

Decals

☐ Name   ☐ Monogram   ☐ Initials

Color _____

Font _____

☐ Quote   ☐ Text   ☐ Image

Color _____

Font _____

Design Details

Design Option	x	Color / Glitter Choices
Solid Color		
Ombre		
Full Glitter		
Half Glitter		

Note

Payment

☐ Cash   ☐ Venmo

☐ Check   ☐ Paypal

☐ Card   ☐ Other

Delivery

☐ Drop Off

☐ Pic Up

☐ Shipping

Pricing

Subtotal _____

Tax _____

Shipping _____

Grand total _____

Deposit _____

Due _____

Tumbler Order Form

Customer	Order N
Address	Order Date
Phone	Due Date
E-mail	Delivery By

Tumbler Details

Tumbler	Size	Quantity

Rush Order   ☐ Yes   ☐ No

Decals

☐ Name   ☐ Monogram   ☐ Initials

Color

Font

☐ Quote   ☐ Text   ☐ Image

Color

Font

Design Details

Design Option	x	Color / Glitter Choices
Solid Color		
Ombre		
Full Glitter		
Half Glitter		

Note

Payment

☐ Cash   ☐ Venmo

☐ Check   ☐ Paypal

☐ Card   ☐ Other

Delivery

☐ Drop Off

☐ Pic Up

☐ Shipping

Pricing

Subtotal

Tax

Shipping

Grand total

Deposit

Due

Tumbler Order Form

Customer _____ Order N _____
Address _____ Order Date _____
Phone _____ Due Date _____
E-mail _____ Delivery By _____

Tumbler Details

Tumbler	Size	Quantity

Rush Order ☐ Yes ☐ No

Decals

☐ Name ☐ Monogram ☐ Initials

Color _____
Font _____

☐ Quote ☐ Text ☐ Image

Color _____
Font _____

Design Details

Design Option	x	Color / Glitter Choices
Solid Color		
Ombre		
Full Glitter		
Half Glitter		

Note

.

Payment

☐ Cash ☐ Venmo
☐ Check ☐ Paypal
☐ Card ☐ Other

Delivery

☐ Drop Off
☐ Pic Up
☐ Shipping

Pricing

Subtotal _____
Tax _____
Shipping _____
Grand total _____
Deposit _____
Due _____

Tumbler Order Form

Customer _____   Order N _____
Address _____   Order Date _____
Phone _____   Due Date _____
E-mail _____   Delivery By _____

Tumbler Details

Tumbler	Size	Quantity

Rush Order   □ Yes   □ No

Decals

□ Name   □ Monogram   □ Initials

Color _____
Font _____

□ Quote   □ Text   □ Image

Color _____
Font _____

Design Details

Design Option	x	Color / Glitter Choices
Solid Color		
Ombre		
Full Glitter		
Half Glitter		

Note

Payment

□ Cash   □ Venmo
□ Check   □ Paypal
□ Card   □ Other

Delivery

□ Drop Off
□ Pic Up
□ Shipping

Pricing

Subtotal _____
Tax _____
Shipping _____
Grand total _____
Deposit _____
Due _____

Tumbler Order Form

Customer		Order N
Address		Order Date
Phone		Due Date
E-mail		Delivery By

Tumbler Details

Tumbler	Size	Quantity

Rush Order ☐ Yes ☐ No

Decals

☐ Name   ☐ Monogram   ☐ Initials

Color _____

Font _____

☐ Quote   ☐ Text   ☐ Image

Color _____

Font _____

Design Details

Design Option	x	Color / Glitter Choices
Solid Color		
Ombre		
Full Glitter		
Half Glitter		

Note

Payment

☐ Cash   ☐ Venmo

☐ Check   ☐ Paypal

☐ Card   ☐ Other

Delivery

☐ Drop Off

☐ Pic Up

☐ Shipping

Pricing

Subtotal	
Tax	
Shipping	
Grand total	
Deposit	
Due	

Tumbler Order Form

Customer _____ Order N _____
Address _____ Order Date _____
Phone _____ Due Date _____
E-mail _____ Delivery By _____

Tumbler Details

Tumbler	Size	Quantity

Rush Order ☐ Yes   ☐ No

Decals

☐ Name ☐ Monogram ☐ Initials

_____

Color _____

Font _____

☐ Quote   ☐ Text   ☐ Image

Color _____

Font _____

Design Details

Design Option	x	Color / Glitter Choices
Solid Color		
Ombre		
Full Glitter		
Half Glitter		

Note

Payment

☐ Cash   ☐ Venmo

☐ Check   ☐ Paypal

☐ Card   ☐ Other

Delivery

☐ Drop Off

☐ Pic Up

☐ Shipping

Pricing

Subtotal _____
Tax _____
Shipping _____
Grand total _____
Deposit _____
Due _____

🥤 Tumbler Order Form 🥤

Customer _____   Order N _____
Address _____   Order Date _____
Phone _____   Due Date _____
E-mail _____   Delivery By _____

Tumbler Details

Tumbler	Size	Quantity

Rush Order   □ Yes   □ No

Decals

□ Name   □ Monogram   □ Initials

Color _____
Font _____

□ Quote   □ Text   □ Image

Color _____
Font _____

Design Details

Design Option	x	Color / Glitter Choices
Solid Color		
Ombre		
Full Glitter		
Half Glitter		

Note

Payment

□ Cash   □ Venmo
□ Check   □ Paypal
□ Card   □ Other

Delivery

□ Drop Off
□ Pic Up
□ Shipping

Pricing

Subtotal _____
Tax _____
Shipping _____
Grand total _____
Deposit _____
Due _____

Tumbler Order Form

Customer _____
Address _____
Phone _____
E-mail _____

Order N _____
Order Date _____
Due Date _____
Delivery By _____

Tumbler Details

Tumbler	Size	Quantity

Rush Order   ☐ Yes   ☐ No

Decals

☐ Name   ☐ Monogram   ☐ Initials

Color _____
Font _____

☐ Quote   ☐ Text   ☐ Image

Color _____
Font _____

Design Details

Design Option	x	Color / Glitter Choices
Solid Color		
Ombre		
Full Glitter		
Half Glitter		

Note

Payment

☐ Cash   ☐ Venmo

☐ Check   ☐ Paypal

☐ Card   ☐ Other

Delivery

☐ Drop Off

☐ Pic Up

☐ Shipping

Pricing

Subtotal _____
Tax _____
Shipping _____
Grand total _____
Deposit _____
Due _____

Tumbler Order Form

Customer _____ Order N _____

Address _____ Order Date _____

Phone _____ Due Date _____

E-mail _____ Delivery By _____

Tumbler Details

Tumbler	Size	Quantity

Rush Order   ☐ Yes   ☐ No

Decals

☐ Name   ☐ Monogram   ☐ Initials

Color _____

Font _____

☐ Quote   ☐ Text   ☐ Image

Color _____

Font _____

Design Details

Design Option	x	Color / Glitter Choices
Solid Color		
Ombre		
Full Glitter		
Half Glitter		

Note

Payment

☐ Cash   ☐ Venmo

☐ Check   ☐ Paypal

☐ Card   ☐ Other

Delivery

☐ Drop Off

☐ Pic Up

☐ Shipping

Pricing

Subtotal _____

Tax _____

Shipping _____

Grand total _____

Deposit _____

Due _____

Tumbler Order Form

Customer		Order N
Address		Order Date
Phone		Due Date
E-mail		Delivery By

Tumbler Details

Tumbler	Size	Quantity

Rush Order ☐ Yes ☐ No

Decals

☐ Name ☐ Monogram ☐ Initials

Color

Font

☐ Quote ☐ Text ☐ Image

Color

Font

Design Details

Design Option	x	Color / Glitter Choices
Solid Color		
Ombre		
Full Glitter		
Half Glitter		

Note

Payment

☐ Cash ☐ Venmo

☐ Check ☐ Paypal

☐ Card ☐ Other

Delivery

☐ Drop Off

☐ Pic Up

☐ Shipping

Pricing

Subtotal

Tax

Shipping

Grand total

Deposit

Due

Tumbler Order Form

Customer _____   Order N _____
Address _____   Order Date _____
Phone _____   Due Date _____
E-mail _____   Delivery By _____

Tumbler Details

Tumbler	Size	Quantity

Rush Order   □ Yes   □ No

Decals

□ Name   □ Monogram   □ Initials

_____

Color _____

Font _____

□ Quote   □ Text   □ Image

_____

Color _____

Font _____

Design Details

Design Option	x	Color / Glitter Choices
Solid Color		
Ombre		
Full Glitter		
Half Glitter		

Note

Payment

□ Cash   □ Venmo

□ Check   □ Paypal

□ Card   □ Other

Delivery

□ Drop Off

□ Pic Up

□ Shipping

Pricing

Subtotal _____
Tax _____
Shipping _____
Grand total _____
Deposit _____
Due _____

Made in the USA
Columbia, SC
01 September 2024